Chronology of Japanese History

装幀 ● 菊地信義
装画 ● 野村俊夫

挿画 ● 大森只光

編集 ● 鈴木節子
編集協力 ● アラン゠キャンベル
翻訳協力 ● 野宮京子

組版 ● parastyle

Published by Kodansha International Ltd.,
17-14, Otowa 1-chome, Bunkyo-ku, Tokyo 112-8652.

First Edition 1999

ISBN4-7700-2453-3
99 00 01 10 9 8 7 6 5 4 3 2 1

バイリンガル日本史年表
Chronology of Japanese History

「英文日本大事典」[編]

本書について
About This Book

■この年表は講談社より刊行された「英文日本大事典」に収められた英文の日本史年表に最新の事項を付け加え、日本語を付け和英のバイリンガル年表にしたものです。「英文日本大事典」の性質上、国際関係の事項が豊富に選ばれています。

This chronology is based on the Chronology of Japanese History that appears in *Japan: An Illustrated Encyclopedia*, published by Kodansha Ltd. Events from recent years have been added along with a Japanese translation in order to create an up-to-date bilingual chronology. One notable feature of the chronology in *Japan: An Illustrated Encyclopedia* that has been carried over to this book is the inclusion of an abundance of entries related to Japan's international contacts.

■事項ごとに上段和文、下段英文で表記し参照しやすくしました。対訳となっており内容は同一です。

For ease of reference, each entry is presented in bilingual format with the Japanese text followed by the equivalent English text.

■日本史用語や作品名など参照しやすくするために、対応する和文・英文のキーワードを太字で示しました。

To make it easier to identify Japanese historical terms, titles of works of art and literature, etc., the corresponding Japanese and English have been highlighted in bold type.

■参考のため世界史上の重要事項もバイリンガルで表記しました。

To help establish context, significant events in world history are also shown in bilingual format.

■巻末には天皇表・年号表・索引なども収録しましたが、これらもすべてバイリンガルになっています。

The supplementary materials at the end of the book include a list of emperors and reigning empresses, a table of Japanese era names, and an index. These, also, are all presented in bilingual format.

■年代はすべて西暦に換算してありますが、1873年1月1日の改暦以前の年月日は、旧暦から西暦に換算しました。旧暦と西暦の年初のずれを考慮して、換算は出来る限り正確に行いました。このため本書における年月日は、時として他書と異なる場合があります。

All dates are shown in Western calendar format. Dates prior to Japan's adoption of the Western calendar on 1 January 1873 have been converted from the old Japanese lunisolar (or lunar-solar) calendar. Every effort has been made to give precise conversions, accounting for the discrepancy between the beginning of the year in the lunisolar calendar and that in the Western solar calendar. Thus the dates given in this book will sometimes differ from those found in many other reference sources.

目次
Contents

日本史年表
CHRONOLOGY OF JAPANESE HISTORY

西暦 Western Calendar	日本史時代区分 Major Periods of Japanese History
	旧石器時代 Paleolithic (pre-10,000 BC)
10,000 BC	縄文時代 Jōmon (ca10,000 BC – ca 300 BC)
300 BC	弥生時代 Yayoi (ca 300 BC – ca AD 300)
AD 300	古墳時代 Kofun (ca 300 – 710)
400	飛鳥時代 Asuka (593 – 710)
500	
600	
700	
800	奈良時代 Nara (710 – 794)
900	
1000	平安時代 Heian (794 – 1185)
1100	藤原時代 Fujiwara (894 – 1185)
1200	
1300	鎌倉時代 Kamakura (1185 – 1333)
1400	室町時代 Muromachi (1333 – 1568)
1500	南北朝時代 Northern and Southern Courts (1337 – 1392)
1600	戦国時代 Sengoku (1467 – 1568)
	安土桃山時代 Azuchi-Momoyama (1568 – 1600)
1700	江戸時代 Edo (1600 – 1868)
1800	
1900	明治時代 Meiji (1868 – 1912)
	大正時代 Taishō (1912 – 1926)
	昭和時代 Shōwa (1926 – 1989)
	平成時代 Heisei (1989 –

旧石器時代 Paleolithic period (pre-10,000 BC)

BC
Before
30,000   旧石器文化：前土器の狩猟採集社会。打製石器をつくる。
Paleolithic culture (*kyūsekki bunka*); crude **stone tools** produced by a preceramic hunting and gathering society.

縄文時代 Jōmon period (ca 10,000 BC – ca 300 BC)

Ca 10,000   縄文土器や磨製石器を製造。縄文時代始まる。
Manufacture of **Jōmon pottery** and polished **stone tools** marks the beginning of the **Jōmon period**.

Ca 5,000   青森県三内丸山に竪穴住居や堀立柱建物の縄文大集落が形成される。
Large Jōmon-period village of **pit houses** and **post-supported buildings** evolves in Sannai Maruyama in Aomori Prefecture.

弥生時代 Yayoi period (ca 300 BC – ca AD 300)

Ca 300   朝鮮半島から水稲耕作が伝わり北九州で弥生文化がはじまる。
Yayoi culture emerges in northern Kyūshū with the introduction of wet-rice cultivation from the Korean Peninsula.

Ca 100   弥生文化、本州中央の関東地方まで広まる。
Yayoi culture reaches the Kantō region in central Honshū.

AD
Ca 1   倭(日本)百余国に分立と中国の歴史書「漢書」に記される。
Japan mentioned in the Chinese historical record *Han shu* (**History of the Former Han Dynasty**) as the land of Wa, composed of a number of states.

57   倭の奴国王中国後漢(25年〜220年)の光武帝に貢を献上し、「漢委奴国王」(金印)の印綬を授与される。
King of the **state of Na** (Nakoku) in Wa offers tribute to Emperor Guangwu of the Chinese Later Han dynasty (25–220) and is awarded the gold seal Kan no Wa no Na no kokuō no in (**seal of the king of the state of Na of Wa of Han**), in return.

Ca 180   倭の諸国、邪馬台国女王卑弥呼の下で統一される。
The various states of Wa join in a league under the headship of Himiko, queen of Yamatai.

239   邪馬台国女王卑弥呼中国の魏に使者を送り、明帝から金印と「親魏倭王」(魏と友好的な倭の支配者)の称号をおくられる。
Himiko, queen of Yamatai, sends an envoy to the kingdom of Wei in China, receiving from Emperor Ming a gold seal and the title *qin wei wowang* (J: *shingi waō*; **Wa ruler friendly to Wei**).

BC

縄文土器 **Jōmon Pottery**

中国で、亀甲文字刻まれる。
Chinese characters engraved on
tortoise shells and animal bones.
仏陀ゴータマ、最初の説法をする。
Historical Buddha Gautama gives
his first sermon.
孔子、子弟の教育をはじめる。
Kong Qiu (known as Confucius in the
West) begins his career as a teacher.

ca 1300

ca 528

ca 520

弥生土器 **Yayoi Pottery**

アレクサンダー大王の東征はじまる。
Alexander the Great begins his
conquest of the East.

334 bc

AD

古墳時代 Kofun period (ca 300–710)

古墳(盛り土をした巨大な墳墓)が造られたのが特徴で、弥生時代以来の農業社会で階層分化が進んだことを示している。古墳の多くは埴輪とよばれる素焼の造形物で飾られていた。大陸から仏教と漢字が伝来し、初の統一政権である大和朝廷が確立した。古墳時代の末期は飛鳥時代(593年〜710年)とよばれ、日本における最初の歴史時代と考えられている。飛鳥時代は大化の改新に代表される制度の改革がすすみ、中国にならった中央集権の体制を確立した。

350	この頃までに現在の奈良県に**大和朝廷**成立。
	By this time the **Yamato court** has been established in what is now Nara Prefecture.
372	朝鮮**百済**の肖古王、倭に使者を送り**七支刀**を献ず。七支刀は現在奈良県石上神宮所蔵。
	Chogo, king of **Paekche** in Korea, sends an emissary to Wa to present a **seven-pronged sword** (*shichishitō*) now held by the Isonokami Shrine in Nara Prefecture.
421	倭王讃、中国の**劉宋王朝**(420年〜479年)に遣使；**倭の五王**時代始まり、劉宋と**梁**(502年〜557年)の皇帝に次々と朝貢。
	Wa ruler San dispatches an embassy to the kindom of the Chinese **Liu-Song dynasty** (420–479); this marks the beginning of the era of the **Five Kings of Wa**, who send emissaries bearing tribute to Liu-Song- and **Liang-dynasty** (502–557) emperors.
527	九州筑紫の国造磐井の乱(527年〜528年)；記録上、**大和朝廷**にたいする最初の反乱。
	Rebellion by Iwai, governor of the province of Tsukushi, Kyūshū (527–528); this is the first recorded rebellion against the **Yamato court**.
538	**百済**の聖明王から仏像と経典を贈られ、はじめて日本に仏教が伝来する。
	Introduction of Buddhism to Japan, when Buddhist images and sutras are sent from Korea by King Sŏng of **Paekche**.
587	仏教の受容をめぐり対立生じる；厩戸皇子(後の**聖徳太子**)に支持された蘇我馬子、反仏教派のリーダー物部守屋を殺害。**蘇我氏**、朝廷支配を確立。
	Factions form for and against the recognition of Buddhism; Soga no Umako, supported by Umayado no Miko (later **Prince Shōtoku**), kills Mononobe no Moriya, leader of the anti-Buddhist faction, and establishes the **Soga family**'s dominance over the court.
592	蘇我馬子、自ら擁立した崇峻天皇を暗殺。
	Soga no Umako engineers the assassination of Emperor Sushun, whose accession he had arranged.

The Kofun period was characterized by the construction of large tomb mounds (*kofun*), indicating the stratification of the agricultural society inherited from the Yayoi period. Many of these tombs were decorated with the hollow clay sculptures known as *haniwa*. The Kofun period witnessed the introduction of Buddhism and the Chinese writing system from the Asian continent and the rise of the Yamato court, a powerful dynasty which established Japan's earliest unified state. The last century of the Kofun period is called the Asuka period (593–710), which is generally considered Japan's first historical age. During this period, a series of institutional innovations, most notably the Taika Reform, created a centralized bureaucratic state based on the Chinese model.

埴輪 **Haniwa**

オドアケル率いるゴート族、西ローマ帝国最後の皇帝ロムルス=アウグストゥルスを廃位。 **476**

Romulus Augustulus, the last emperor of the Western Roman Empire, deposed by the Goths under Odoacer.

中国に隋王朝(589年〜618年)はじまる。 **589**

Beginning of the Sui dynasty (589–618) in China.

観音山古墳(群馬県)の埴輪配置
Haniwa Placement at the 6th-century Kannon'yama Tomb in Gumma Prefecture

横穴式石室 corridor-type stone chamber

— 円筒埴輪推定配置地点 presumed location of *haniwa* cylinders
□○ 形象・円筒埴輪発掘地点 excaved *haniwa* sculptures and cylinders

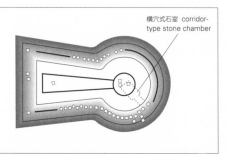

593　聖徳太子、女帝推古天皇から摂政に任命される。
Prince Shōtoku appointed regent by **Empress Suiko**.

600　隋王朝(589年～618年)へ最初の**遣隋使**派遣。
First **embassy to Sui-dynasty** (589–618) China (*kenzuishi*) dispatched.

604　「冠位十二階」制定。聖徳太子「十七条憲法」を公布。
Kan'i jūnikai (**"twelve grades of cap rank"**) system of court ranks instituted. Prince Shōtoku promulgates **Seventeen-Article Constitution**.

607　小野妹子第2次遣隋使に任命される。
Ono no Imoko appointed leader of the second embassy to Sui China.
　　法隆寺の造営終わる。
Construction of the Buddhist temple Hōryūji completed.

620　聖徳太子と蘇我馬子、史書「天皇記」と「国記」を編纂と伝えられるが現存せず。
Prince Shōtoku and Soga no Umako said to have compiled the histories *Tennōki* (**Record of the Emperors**) and *Kokki* (**Record of the Nation**), no longer extant.

630　唐王朝(618年～907年)へ第1次**遣唐使**派遣。
First **embassy to Tang-dynasty** (618–907) China (*kentōshi*) dispatched.

645　中大兄皇子(後の天智天皇)と中臣鎌足(後の藤原鎌足)、蘇我氏を滅ぼし**大化の改新**始まる。
Prince Naka no Ōe (later Emperor Tenji) and Nakatomi no Kamatari (later Fujiwara no Kamatari) destroy the Soga Family and initiate the **Taika Reform**.
　　「大化」元年；**年号**の制度始まる。
First year of the Taika era; use of **era names** (*nengō*) instituted.

663　百済救援のために派遣された倭国軍、朝鮮半島南西岸**白村江の戦い**で**新羅**と同盟を結んだ唐の水軍に敗れる。
Japanese forces sent to aid the Korean kingdom of **Paekche** are defeated in the **Battle of Hakusonkō** (Hakusukinoe) off the southwestern coast of the Korean Peninsula by a Tang Chinese fleet allied with the Korean kingdom of **Silla**.

667　中大兄皇子(後の天智天皇)、琵琶湖の南西岸に大津宮を造営。672年まで都となる。
Imperial palace Ōtsu no Miya established by Prince Naka no Ōe (later Emperor Tenji) on the southwestern shore of Lake Biwa. Capital until 672.

668　**新羅**の朝鮮統一により百済と**高句麗**から日本への移住者(渡来人)が増加。
Unification of Korea by the kingdom of **Silla** spurs immigration to Japan by refugees from Paekche and **Koguryŏ** (*toraijin*).

672　**壬申の乱**：大海人皇子(後の天武天皇)、甥で皇位継承者の大友皇子から皇位を奪い、飛鳥浄御原宮に皇室を造営。
Jinshin Disturbance: Prince Ōama (later Emperor Temmu) usurps the throne from his nephew and designated heir Prince Ōtomo; establishes residence at Asuka Kiyomihara no Miya.

聖徳太子 **Prince Shōtoku**

予言者マホメット、メディナ到着。イス　**622**
ラム暦元年。
Prophet Muhammad arrives in
Medina; the Islamic Era begins.

唐王朝(618年〜907年)中国統一。　**624**
China unified under the Tang
dynasty (618–907).

新羅、唐と同盟して朝鮮を統一；676年　**668**
唐、半島より追放される。
Silla unifies Korea with the assistance
of Tang China; the Chinese are
driven out of the peninsula in 676.

684 八色の姓制定。氏に姓を授与し、天皇を頂点とするピラミッド型の階層制
を形成。

System of eight cognomens (*yakusa no kabane*) instituted, under
which members of **lineage groups** (*uji*) are assigned titles of rank,
forming a social pyramid with the emperor at its apex.

694 藤原京を都とする。710年まで都となる。

Capital city Fujiwarakyō established. Capital until 710.

701 刑法と行政法(**律令**)の**大宝律令**の編纂が完了する；翌年施行。

Compilation of the **Taihō Code** of penal and **administrative laws**
(*ritsuryō*) completed; becomes effective the following year.

708 「和同開珎」の鋳造開始；富本銭とともに日本で鋳造された最初の硬貨の1つ。

Minting of the Wadō *kaichin* initiated; it is one of the first coinages
(along with the *fuhonsen*) minted in Japan.

奈良時代 Nara period (710–794)

平城京(奈良)に都がおかれた時代。中国の影響で始まった律令政治が成熟
期を迎え、さまざまな中国の文化や技術を積極的に採り入れた。仏教が国
教として認められ、中央集権の権威を示すために日本全国に寺院が建設さ
れた。天平文化の名で知られる芸術が花開き、最古の編年記「古事記」や
「日本書紀」、和歌集「万葉集」が編まれた。

710 平城京(奈良)を都とする。784年まで都となる。

Capital city Heijōkyō (Nara) established. Capital until 784.

712 太安万侶、現存する日本最古の編年体の歴史物語「**古事記**」を撰上。

Compilation of the historical narrative *Kojiki* (**Record of Ancient
Matters**), Japan's oldest extant chronicle, is completed by Ō no
Yasumaro.

720 歴史物語「**日本書紀**」(「日本紀」ともいう)完成。

Historical narrative *Nihon shoki* (**Chronicle of Japan**; also known as
the *Nihongi*) completed.

723 三世一身の法発布；**班田収授法**で禁止されていた開墾地の私的所有を初め
て公に認める。

Sanze Isshin no Hō (**Laws of Three Generations or a Lifetime**) put
into effect; this marks the first government recognition of private
ownership of reclaimed lands, which had been prohibited under the
handen shūju system (**land allotment system**).

The establishment of the capital city Heijōkyō (Nara) marked the beginning of the Nara period, which was characterized by the maturation of the Chinese-inspired *ritsuryō* system of government and the active adoption of other aspects of Chinese culture and technology. Buddhism gained official recognition as the state religion, and temples were constructed throughout Japan in an effort to buttress the authority of the central state. This period also saw the flowering of the arts known as Tempyō culture, the compilation of Japan's first historical chronicles, the *Kojiki* and *Nihon shoki*, and the first of the great anthologies of Japanese poetry, the *Man'yōshū*.

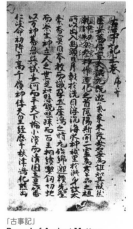

「古事記」
Record of Ancient Matters

724 蝦夷に対する防衛と侵略の軍事拠点として、陸奥国に多賀の柵(後の多賀城)が建設される。

Taga no Ki (later known as Tagajō) established in **Mutsu Province** as a military outpost from which defensive operations and forays against the Ezo tribesmen are mounted.

727 北アジアの渤海の使者、初来日。

First embassy from the north Asian kingdom of **Bohai** (Po-hai) arrives in Japan.

733 「出雲国風土記」完成。

Regional gazetteer *Izumo no kuni fudoki* completed.

741 聖武天皇、諸国に国分寺と国分尼寺建立の詔を出す。

Emperor Shōmu decrees construction of two state temples, a *kokubunji* (**provincial temple**) and a *kokubunniji* (**provincial nunnery**), in each province.

743 墾田永年私財法公布；開墾した田地の永久私有を認め、荘園の法的根拠となる。

Konden Einen Shizai Hō promulgated; recognizing the permanent privatization of reclaimed land, this law lays the legal basis for the emergence of the **landed estates** called *shōen*.

詔勅により東大寺巨大仏像(大仏)の造立始まる；752年完成。

Construction of a huge Buddha image (*daibutsu*) at the temple Tōdaiji initiated by imperial decree; it is completed in 752.

751 「懐風藻」成立；日本人の歌人による現存最古の漢詩集。

Kaifūsō (**Verses in Memory of Poets Past**) compiled; it is the oldest extant collection of Chinese poetry by Japanese poets.

754 仏僧鑑真、中国より渡来。

Buddhist priest **Jianzhen** (J: Ganjin) arrives in Japan from China.

756 光明皇后、夫の故聖武天皇およびその朝廷で使われていた貴重な遺愛の品600余を東大寺に献納。このうち100点余が正倉院宝物の中核をなす。

Empress Kōmyō donates to the temple Tōdaiji some 600 valuable objects used by her late husband Emperor Shōmu and his court; more than 100 of these objects become the core of the **Shōsoin treasure house collection**.

759 鑑真、唐招提寺創建。

Jianzhen (J: Ganjin) founds the temple Tōshōdaiji.

現存最古の和歌集「万葉集」この頃完成。

The *Man'yōshū* (**Collection of Ten Thousand Leaves**), the oldest extant anthology of Japanese poetry, is completed around this time.

784 長岡京に遷都。794年まで都がおかれる。

Capital moved to Nagaokakyō. Capital until 794.

788 天台宗開祖最澄、延暦寺を建立。

Saichō, founder of the **Tendai sect** of Buddhism, establishes the temple Enryakuji on Mt. Hiei.

奈良大仏 **Great Buddha of Nara**

唐の詩人李白・杜甫が活躍。
Tang poets Li Bo and Du Fu active.

ca 750

正倉院 **Shōsōin**

平安時代 Heian period (794–1185)

平安京(京都)遷都とともにはじまる平安時代は中国伝来の文化が十分に消化吸収されて、国風の貴族文化が花開いた。仮名文字が発展して日本固有の文学の伝統が生まれ、日本文学を代表する紫式部の大作「源氏物語」が生まれた。平安時代の政治は藤原氏一族の摂政・関白による朝廷支配によって特徴づけられる。またこの時代は地方の武士が力を増し荘園が全国に広がって、中央集権国家の律令制度の崩壊をもたらした。

794　平安京(京都)遷都。1868年まで都がおかれる。

Capital moved to Heiankyō (Kyōto). Capital until 1868.

801　坂上田村麻呂、蝦夷征討のため東北に派遣される。

Sakanoue no Tamuramaro sets out on a campaign in the north against the Ezo tribesmen.

810　薬子の変：藤原北家、朝廷で政治権力を確立。

Kusuko Incident: the **Hokke branch of the Fujiwara family** gains political ascendancy at the imperial court.

823　真言宗の開祖空海、本山となる東寺の管長に任命される。

Kūkai, founder of the **Shingon sect** of Buddhism, appointed abbot of Tōji, which becomes the sect's head temple.

866　応天門の変：藤原良房、皇族以外で初めて摂政となり(摂関政治の基礎を築く)、政敵を滅ぼす。

Ōtemmon Conspiracy: Fujiwara no Yoshifusa establishes himself as the first non-royal holder of the office of regent (thus laying the foundations for the system of **regency government**) and destroys his political rivals.

903　歌人であり政治家でもある菅原道真、配所の太宰府にて没する；2年前、謀叛の冤罪で告発された。

Poet and political figure Sugawara no Michizane dies in exile in Dazaifu; he had been falsely accused two years earlier of plotting against the throne.

905　第1代勅撰和歌集「古今和歌集」成立。

The *Kokin wakashū* (**Collection from Ancient and Modern Times**), the first **imperial anthology** of *waka* verse, is completed.

935　紀貫之、仮名文字の紀行文「土佐日記」を書く。

Ki no Tsurayuki composes the *Tosa nikki* (tr *The Tosa Diary*), a poetical **travel diary** written in the native *kana* syllabary.

938　浄土教の布教で知られる仏僧空也、京都で念仏を唱え始める。

The Buddhist monk Kūya, known for his popularization of **Pure Land Buddhism**, begins chanting the *nembutsu* (the invocation **Namu Amida Butsu**) in the streets of Kyōto.

The Heian period, which began with the establishment of the imperial capital at Heiankyō (Kyōto), saw the full assimilation of Chinese influences and the flowering of an indigenous aristocratic culture. The development of the Japanese *kana* syllabary gave birth to a truly native literary tradition, including some of the finest works of Japanese poetry and prose, such as Murasaki Shikibu's masterpiece, the *Tale of Genji*. Politically, the Heian period was characterized by the domination of the imperial court by regents of the Fujiwara family. This age also witnessed the growing power of provincial warrior bands and the proliferation of private estates (*shōen*), which together brought about the disintegration of the *ritsuryō* system of centralized government.

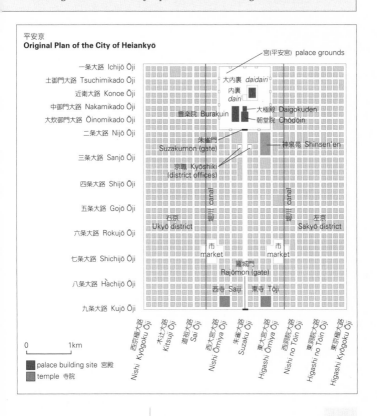

平安京
Original Plan of the City of Heiankyō

940	常陸国で平将門の乱；擡頭する武士階級による最初の大きな反乱。

Rebellion by Taira no Masakado in **Hitachi Province**; this is the first major rebellion of the rising warrior class against the government.

974 この頃「蜻蛉日記」完成。作者は藤原道綱の母。

Approximate date of completion of the *Kagerō nikki* (tr *The Gossamer Years*), the diary of a lady who is known as the mother of Fujiwara no Michitsuna.

985 僧源信、経論集「往生要集」を完成；これにより貴族の間に浄土教が広まる。

The Buddhist monk Genshin completes the religious tract *Ōjōyōshū* **(The Essentials of Pure Land Rebirth)**; the work contributes to the spread of **Pure Land Buddhism** among the aristocracy.

995 藤原道長、藤原氏の氏長者となる；藤原氏による朝廷支配の黄金時代始まる。

Fujiwara no Michinaga becomes head of the **Fujiwara family**; the golden age of its domination of the imperial court begins.

996 清少納言「枕草子」の一部が流布する；当時の朝廷貴族の価値観や美意識をいきいきと伝える洗練された随筆。

A portion of Sei Shōnagon's *Makura no sōshi* (tr *The Pillow Book of Sei Shōnagon*) is now in circulation; this elegant volume of brief prose sketches brings alive the social and aesthetic values of the court aristocracy.

1008 「紫式部日記」によると「源氏物語」主要部分、この頃までに完成。

Entry in Murasaki Shikibu's diary indicates that a substantial part of the *Genji monogatari* (tr *Tale of Genji*), has now been written.

1051 前9年の役(1051年～1062年)、陸奥国で始まる。安倍頼時父子を攻撃。

Earlier Nine Years' War (1051–62) begins in **Mutsu Province**. Military campaign waged against Abe no Yoritoki and his sons.

1053 平等院鳳凰堂落成；本尊の「阿弥陀如来」は定朝作。

Construction of the Hōōdō **(Phoenix Hall)**, dedicated to the **Buddha Amida**, completed at the temple Byōdōin; Jōchō sculpts its main icon.

1059 この頃「更級日記」完成；作者は菅原孝標女。

Probable date of completion of the *Sarashina nikki* (tr *As I Crossed a Bridge of Dreams*); the author was a lady known as the daughter of Sugawara Takasue.

1083 後3年の役(1083年～1087年)、奥羽の清原氏を攻撃。

Later Three Years' War (1083–87) begins against the **Kiyohara family** in Dewa and Mutsu provinces.

1087 白河天皇退位、院政を開始する。

Emperor Shirakawa abdicates, establishes the system of "**cloister government**" (*insei*).

1156 保元の乱：朝廷において平氏と源氏の権力抗争、はじまる。

Hōgen Disturbance: rivalry between the **Taira family** and the **Minamoto family** for political power at court begins.

1160 平治の乱(平治元年12月)：平氏、朝廷において権力を確立する。

Heiji Disturbance (Heiji 1.12): influence of the **Taira family** over the imperial court established.

1175 法然、京都で説法をはじめる。浄土宗開基。

Hōnen begins to preach in Kyōto and founds the **Jōdo sect** of Buddhism.

平清盛 **Taira no Kiyomori**

シャルルマーニュ、教皇レオ3世の手に **800**
より西ローマ帝国皇帝として戴冠する。
Charlemagne crowned by Pope Leo
III as Charles I, emperor of the Holy
Roman Empire.

王建、高麗を建国して朝鮮半島を支配。 **935**
Wang Kŏn establishes the hegemony
of the kingdom of Koryŏ over the
Korean Peninsula.

中国に北宋(960年～1126年)はじまる。 **960**
Beginning of the Northern Song
dynasty (960–1126) in China.

「紫式部日記絵巻」
Scroll of the Lady Murasaki's Diary

ノルマンディー公ウィリアム、ヘースティ **1066**
ィングズの戦いでハロルド王を敗りイン
グランド王となる。
William, duke of Normandy, defeats
King Harold at the Battle of Hastings
and is crowned king of England.

「平治物語絵巻」 **Tale of Heiji Scrolls**

中国に南宋(1127年～1279年)はじまる。 **1127**
Beginning of the Southern Song
dynasty (1127–1279) in China.

クメール君主スールヤヴァルマン2世、 **ca 1150**
大伽藍アンコール＝ワットを建立する。
Khmer monarch Suryavarman II
completes the temple complex of
Angkor Wat.

オックスフォード大学創立。 **ca 1167**
Oxford University established.

1180

平清盛の孫、安徳天皇即位。

Taira no Kiyomori's grandson accedes as Emperor Antoku.

源頼政、源頼朝、源義仲が平清盛に対して挙兵；**源平の争乱**(治承・寿永の乱)始まる。

Minamoto no Yorimasa, Minamoto no Yoritomo, and Minamoto no Yoshinaka rise against the forces of Kiyomori; the **Taira-Minamoto War** (also known as the **Disturbances during the Chishō and Juei eras**) begins.

1183

源義仲、平氏を敗り入京；平氏は都を落ち西国に逃れる。

Minamoto no Yoshinaka defeats the Taira army and enters Kyōto; Taira forces abandon Kyōto and retreat to southwestern Honshū.

鎌倉時代 Kamakura period (1185–1333)

源平の争乱における源頼朝の勝利は鎌倉時代の幕開けを告げ、地方武士階級の政治的進出のはじまりでもあった。頼朝による守護・地頭の任命は、19世紀半ばまで続く武家政権の最初となる鎌倉幕府の基礎を固めた。また北条氏が権力を確立したほか、蒙古の襲来や禅宗の伝来もみられた。仏教の新宗派が生まれて庶民の間に信仰が広まったのも鎌倉時代に入ってからである。

1185

源義経、**壇ノ浦の戦い**で平氏を滅ぼす；兄、源頼朝は日本の最高権力者となる。

Minamoto no Yoshitsune annihilates the Taira army in the **Battle of Dannoura**; his brother Minamoto no Yoritomo is now the most powerful figure in Japan.

源頼朝、**守護**(地方警察官)・**地頭**(領地管理人)設置の勅許を受け、1180年鎌倉に開いた武家政権(後の**鎌倉幕府**)を全国に拡大、強化する。

Minamoto no Yoritomo receives from the imperial court the right to appoint **provincial constables** (*shugo*) and **estate stewards** (*jitō*), consolidating and extending nationwide the warrior governmental organization (later known as the **Kamakura shogunate**) that he had established at Kamakura in 1180.

1189

源頼朝、**奥州藤原氏**を滅ぼし、奥州を制圧する。

Minamoto no Yoritomo destroys the **Ōshū Fujiwara family**, gains control over northeastern Japan.

1191

栄西、中国で4年間学んで帰国。禅宗**臨済宗**を開き中国の禅の教えを広め始める。

Eisai, the founder of the **Rinzai sect** of Zen Buddhism in Japan, returns from four years of study in China and begins to advocate Chinese Zen teachings in Japan.

「源平合戦図屏風」
Folding Screens of Taira-Minamoto War

Minamoto no Yoritomo's victory in the Taira-Minamoto War (Gempei no Sōran) heralded the beginning of the Kamakura period and the rise to political power of the provincial warrior class. His appointment of provincial governors (*shugo*) and estate stewards (*jitō*) established the foundations of the Kamakura shogunate, the first in a series of military governments that would rule Japan until the mid-19th century. Other developments of this period included the eventual political ascendancy of the Hōjō family, the Mongol Invasions of Japan, the introduction of Zen Buddhism, and the emergence of new popular sects that spread the Buddhist religion among the common people.

源頼朝 **Minamoto no Yoritomo**

1192　後鳥羽天皇、源頼朝を征夷大将軍に任命。

Minamoto no Yoritomo appointed *seii tai shōgun* ("**barbarian-subduing generalissimo**") by Emperor Go-Toba.

1199　源頼朝、没する；北条氏、鎌倉幕府を支配する。

Minamoto no Yoritomo dies; **Hōjō family** achieves control of the **Kamakura shogunate**.

1203　北条時政執権となる。

Hōjō Tokimasa assumes the office of **shogunal regent** (*shikken*).

慶派の快慶、運慶等奈良東大寺南大門の仁王像を造立。

Kaikei, Unkei, and other members of the **Kei school** sculpt the pair of guardian deities housed in the **Great South Gate** at the temple Tōdaiji in Nara.

1205　「新古今和歌集」撰進される；「古今和歌集」後の最も重要な勅撰和歌集。

The *Shin kokin wakashū* (**New Collection from Ancient and Modern Times**), the most important of the imperial anthologies of *waka* poetry after the *Kokin wakashū*, is submitted to the throne.

1212　鴨長明、代表作の瞑想的随筆「方丈記」を完成。

Kamo no Chōmei completes his masterwork, the contemplative essay *Hōjōki* (tr *An Account of My Hut*).

1218　この頃までに、「平家物語」の原型完成。

Early versions of the *Heike monogatari* (tr *The Tale of the Heike*) in existence by about this time.

1219　源実朝暗殺され源氏の将軍絶える。北条氏の執権支配が続く。

Minamoto no Sanetomo assassinated, ending the line of Minamoto shōguns. Members of the Hōjō family continue to rule as regents.

1221　承久の乱：後鳥羽上皇と順徳上皇、幕府によって退位・流罪に処せられる。

Jōkyū Disturbance: abdicated emperors Go-Toba and Juntoku sent into exile by the shogunate.

1224　親鸞、主著「教行信証」この頃一応完成。これをもって浄土真宗開基とする。

Shinran thought to have completed the earliest version of his major work, the *Kyōgyōshinshō* (**A Collection of Passages Revealing the True Teaching, Practice, and Attainment of the Pure Land**); this event is considered to mark his founding of the **Jōdo Shin sect** of Buddhism.

1226　執権北条泰時、評定衆を置く；幕府は合議制となる。

Hyōjōshū (**Council of State**) established by **shogunal regent** Hōjō Yasutoki; this institutes government by council.

1227　道元禅宗の一派曹洞宗を開く。

Dōgen establishes the **Sōtō sect** of Zen Buddhism.

1232　御成敗式目制定：最初の武家法典。

Goseibai Shikimoku (**The Formulary of Adjudications**) promulgated; it is the first codification of warrior house law.

1242　四条天皇没するが皇嗣なく、幕府は後嵯峨天皇を擁立；後嵯峨天皇の2人の皇子（後の後深草天皇と亀山天皇）は皇位をめぐって対立、南北朝成立（1337年）の原因となる。

Emperor Shijō dies without an heir, and the shogunate intercedes to force the accession of Emperor Go-Saga; Go-Saga's princes, who

仁王 **Benevolent King**

印刷術、中国で広まる。
Printing spreads in China.

ca 1200

英王ジョン「マグナカルタ」を承認。
Magna Carta issued, under duress,
by King John of England.

1215

モンゴル人、ポーランドとハンガリーを
侵略。
Mongols invade Poland and
Hungary.

1240

御成敗式目 **Goseibai Shikimoku**

later become the emperors Go-Fukakusa and Kameyama, initiate the succession dispute that culminates in 1337 in the establishment of the **Northern and Southern Courts**.

1252	鎌倉高徳院で巨大な阿弥陀仏座像・鎌倉大仏の建立が始まる。

Construction of the Kamakura Daibutsu, a giant seated image of the Buddha Amida, begins at the temple Kōtokuin in Kamakura.

1253 日蓮、日蓮宗を開く。

Nichiren establishes the **Nichiren sect** of Buddhism.

1274 文永の役：第1回蒙古襲来。

Bun'ei Expedition: first of the **Mongol invasions of Japan**.

1281 弘安の役：第2回蒙古襲来。

Kōan Expedition: second of the **Mongol invasions of Japan**.

1297 鎌倉幕府、徳政令公布；御家人の所領が高利貸業者に渡るのを防ぐため、借金を取り消す。

Tokusei **(cancellation of debts) decree** issued by the Kamakura shogunate: debts canceled to protect shogunal retainers from the alienation of their lands to creditors.

1318 後醍醐天皇即位。

Emperor Go-Daigo ascends the throne.

1324 正中の変；後醍醐天皇、鎌倉幕府打倒をめざすが、失敗に終わる。

Shōchū Conspiracy, led by Emperor Go-Daigo against the Kamakura shogunate, fails.

1330 この頃吉田兼好の代表作、随筆集「徒然草」完成。

Yoshida Kenkō completes his masterwork, the collection of essays *Tsurezuregusa* (tr *Essays in Idleness*), around this time.

1331 元弘の変；後醍醐天皇、再び倒幕を企てるが失敗、翌年隠岐島へ流される。

Genkō Incident: Emperor Go-Daigo fails a second time to wrest power from the Kamakura shogunate; he is exiled to the island of Oki the following year.

室町時代 Muromachi period (1333–1568)

足利尊氏が鎌倉幕府を滅ぼし、室町時代がはじまる。文化は大いに発展したが、社会的には不安定な時代であった。室町時代に入って数十年間、幕府は南北朝の抗争で混乱した。また幕府は守護大名を制御することが出来ず、応仁の乱以後は完全に衰退し、戦国時代(1467年～1568年)と呼ばれる内乱の100年へと突入していく。しかし同時に室町時代は能や狂言などの新しい形式の芸術や、禅の影響を受けた茶の湯・華道・水墨画の発達が見られた。

マルコ=ポーロ、フビライ=ハーンのモ **1271**
ンゴル(元)へ旅立つ。

Marco Polo sets out on his journey to
the court of the Mongol emperor
Kublai Khan.

フビライ=ハーン、南宋を滅ぼし中国に **1279**
元朝(1279年〜1368年)を開く。

Kublai Khan conquers the Southern
Song and establishes the Yuan
dynasty (1279–1368) in China.

蒙古襲来ルート
Routes of the Mongol Invasions

- - - 文永の役
invasion route in 1274
弘安の役
invasion routes in 1281
—— 東路軍
Eastern Route Army
...... 江南軍
Southern Route Army

朝鮮 Korea

朝鮮海峡 Korea Strait

対馬 Tsushima

対馬海峡 Tsushima Strait

玄界灘 Genkai Sea

寧波 from Ningbo

壱岐島 Iki

博多 Hakata

九州 Kyūshū

The destruction of the Kamakura shogunate by the forces of
Ashikaga Takauji signified the beginning of the Muromachi period,
an era of great cultural achievement and persistent social instability.
The first decades of the Muromachi shogunate were disrupted by
conflict between the Northern and Southern Courts. The shogunate
was unable to restrain the ambitions of powerful provincial
governors (*shugo daimyō*) and collapsed entirely after the Ōnin War,
which ushered in a century of civil strife known as the Sengoku
period (1467–1568). At the same time, the Muromachi period saw the
impressive development of new artistic forms such as Nō and
kyōgen, as well as Zen-inspired arts such as the tea ceremony, flower
arrangement, and ink printing.

1333　建武の中興(建武の新政)。鎌倉幕府滅亡；後醍醐天皇が復権する。

Kemmu Restoration: **Kamakura shogunate** collapses; power restored to Emperor Go-Daigo.

1335　足利尊氏、後醍醐天皇に背く。

Ashikaga Takauji turns against Emperor Go-Daigo.

1336　湊川の戦い：足利尊氏、新田義貞と楠木正成の皇軍を敗って入京；後醍醐天皇から三種の神器を授受された豊仁親王を光明天皇として擁立。後醍醐天皇は花山院に幽閉される。

Battle of Minatogawa: Ashikaga Takauji defeats the imperial loyalist armies of Nitta Yoshisada and Kusunoki Masashige and enters Kyōto; Takauji forces Emperor Go-Daigo to relinquish the **imperial regalia** (mirror, sword, and jewels) to Prince Toyohito, installs the latter as Emperor Kōmyō, and confines Go-Daigo at the Kazan Palace.

足利尊氏幕府の施政方針を定めた建武式目を公布。

The Kemmu Shikimoku, a code of governmental principles, is promulgated by Ashikaga Takauji.

1337　後醍醐天皇、豊仁親王に授受した神器の正当性を否定、退位を拒んで吉野に赴き南朝を設立する。南北朝時代始まる。

Emperor Go-Daigo escapes to Yoshino; declaring that the regalia he had surrendered to Prince Toyohito were imitations and denying his abdication, he establishes the Southern Court. It marks the beginning of the period of **Northern and Southern Courts**.

1338　足利尊氏、北朝より征夷大将軍に任じられ室町幕府はじまる。

Ashikaga Takauji receives the title of *seii tai shōgun* ("**barbarian-subduing generalissimo**") from the Northern Court, founds the **Muromachi shogunate**.

1343　北畠親房、南朝の正統性を説く歴史書「神皇正統記」を書き終える。

Kitabatake Chikafusa concludes his *Jinnō shōtō ki* (**Chronicle of the Direct Descent of Divine Sovereigns**), a historical tract designed to support the Southern Court.

1350　観応の擾乱(1350年〜1352年)：足利直義、兄の将軍足利尊氏に反乱。

Kannō Disturbance (1350–52): Ashikaga Tadayoshi rebels against his brother, the shōgun Ashikaga Takauji.

1356　二条良基と救済、連歌集「菟玖波集」の編集を始める。

Nijō Yoshimoto and Gusai begin compilation of the *renga* (**linked verse**) collection *Tsukubashū*.

1370　この頃から日本の海賊(倭寇)船団、中国や朝鮮高麗の沿岸地域を略奪する。

From around this time fleets of **Japanese pirates** (*wakō*) pillage coastal areas of China and the Korean kingdom of **Koryŏ**.

1391　明徳の乱(1391年〜1392年)：山名氏、幕府の支配を脅かすが将軍足利義満に敗れる。

Meitoku Rebellion (1391–92): the **Yamana family** threatens shogunal ascendancy and is defeated by the shōgun Ashikaga Yoshimitsu.

1392　後小松天皇のもと南北両朝合体。

Northern and Southern Courts reconciled with the acceptance of Emperor Go-Komatsu as sole sovereign.

「倭寇図巻」 Scroll of Wakō

英仏百年戦争はじまる。 **1337**
Hundred Years' War, waged by
England against France, begins.

ヨーロッパで黒死病流行(1347年〜1351 **1347**
年)。
Black Death rages in Europe (1347–
51).

朱元璋、中国に明(1368年〜1644年)を建 **1368**
国する。
Zhu Yuanzhang founds the Ming
dynasty (1368–1644) in China.

朝鮮で李成桂、王を称し李王朝(1392年 **1392**
〜1910年)をたてる。
Yi Sŏng-gye declares himself king of
Korea, founds the Yi dynasty (1392–
1910).

1397 将軍足利義満、京都に金閣寺(正式名称鹿苑寺)の造営はじめる。

Shōgun Ashikaga Yoshimitsu begins construction of the temple Kinkakuji (**Temple of the Golden Pavillion**; formally known as Rokuonji) in Kyōto.

1399 応永の乱(1399年～1400年)：有力な守護大名大内氏、将軍足利義満に敗れる。

Ōei Rebellion (1399–1400): the powerful *shugo daimyō* **Ōuchi family** defeated by the shōgun Ashikaga Yoshimitsu.

1400 世阿弥能楽論書「風姿花伝」第1編～3編を執筆。

Zeami completes the first three chapters of his *Fūshi kaden* (**Transmission of the Flower of Acting Style**), a treatise on Nō drama.

1401 将軍足利義満、中国の明朝(1368年～1644年)に使者を送る；翌年、外交関係が確立。

Shōgun Ashikaga Yoshimitsu sends an envoy to **Ming-dynasty** (1368–1644) China; diplomatic relations established the following year.

1404 中国明朝(1368年～1644年)との勘合貿易はじまる。

Tally trade initiated with Ming-dynasty (1368–1644) China.

1415 琉球王国、日本と中継貿易を始める。

Ryūkyū Kingdom establishes entrepôt trade with Japan.

1419 応永の外冠：朝鮮の李王朝(1392年～1910年)、倭寇の根拠地対馬に船隊を送り襲撃する。

Ōei Invasion: fleet dispatched by **Yi-dynasty** (1392–1910) Korea attacks pirate (*wakō*) base on the Japanese island of Tsushima.

1428 土一揆：京都とその周辺で農民が反乱；債務の取消(徳政)を要求。

Tsuchi ikki: **peasant uprising** in Kyōto and surrounding provinces; **cancellation of debts** (*tokusei*) sought.

1441 赤松満祐、将軍足利義教を暗殺。

Akamatsu Mitsusuke assassinates the shōgun Ashikaga Yoshinori.

1467 応仁の乱(1467年～1477年)はじまる；京都荒廃。

Ōnin War begins (1467–1477); Kyōto laid waste.

1471 仏僧蓮如、越前国吉崎に改宗道場を設立；北陸地方に浄土真宗広まる。

Buddhist monk Rennyo establishes base for proselytizing in Yoshizaki, **Echizen Province**; as a result of his efforts the **Jōdo Shin sect** spreads through the Hokuriku region.

1483 足利義政譲位して京都東山の山荘(後の銀閣寺；正式には慈照寺)に移る。東山を中心に東山文化栄える。

Retired shōgun Ashikaga Yoshimasa settles at the villa that later becomes the temple Ginkakuji (**Temple of the Silver Pavillion**; formally known as Jishōji); located in the Higashiyama section of Kyōto, this becomes known as the center of **Higashiyama culture**.

1486 山城国一揆：国人・地侍らが、山城地方を支配する。

Yamashiro no Kuni Ikki: a league of *kokujin* (**local *samurai* proprietors**) and *jizamurai* (**yeoman warriors**) gains control over much of Yamashiro Province.

1488 宗祇・肖柏・宗長、連歌百句の大作「水無瀬三吟百韻」を詠む。

Sōgi, Shōhaku, and Sōchō compose the hundred-link poem *Minase sangin hyakuin* (**One Hundred Links by Three Poets at Minase**), a masterpiece of *renga*.

足利義満 **Ashikaga Yoshimitsu**

G=チョーサー、「カンタベリ物語」を未完のまま没する。

Geoffrey Chaucer dies before completing *The Canterbury Tales*.

1400

J=グーテンベルグ「42行聖書」完成；ヨーロッパにおける最初の活版印刷本。

Johannes Gutenberg completes the Forty-Two Line Bible, the earliest book printed in Europe from movable type.

Ca 1445

銀閣寺
Temple of the Silver Pavillion

一向一揆：浄土真宗門徒(一向宗徒)加賀国の守護勢を打破して、支配権を
にぎる。

Ikkō *ikki*: adherents of the **Jōdo Shin sect** of Buddhism vanquish the
army of the **governor** (*shugo*) of **Kaga Province** and establish
autonomous rule there.

1495   水墨画家雪舟等楊、代表作「破墨山水図」作成。

Ink painter Sesshū Tōyō produces his best-known work, *Haboku
sansuizu* (**Haboku Landscape**).

1523   細川氏と大内氏の勘合船、中国の寧波で、明朝(1368年〜1644年)との勘合
貿易の権利をめぐって衝突；その後大内氏が貿易を独占。

Envoys of the **Hosokawa family** and the **Ōuchi family** clash in
Ningbo, China, over rights to **tally trade** with Ming-dynasty
(1368–1644) China; the Ōuchi family gains the monopoly.

1536   天文法華の乱：日蓮宗信徒による京都の自治組織(法華一揆)が、天台宗延
暦寺の僧兵に攻められ壊滅する。

Tembun Hokke Rebelliion: an autonomous government
established in Kyōto by adherents of the **Nichiren sect** (Hokke *ikki*)
is brought to a violent end by **warrior-monks** of the **Tendai sect**
temple Enryakuji.

この頃から倭冦、中国明(1368年〜1644年)の沿岸から内陸にかけて略奪する。

From around this time **Japanese pirates** (*wakō*) pillage coastal and
inland areas of **Ming-dynasty** (1368–1644) China.

1543   ポルトガル人、種子島に火縄銃を伝える。

Matchlock muskets (*hinawajū*) are introduced to Japan by the
Portuguese on the island of Tanegashima off the coast of Kyūshū.

1549   フランシスコ＝ザビエル、鹿児島において日本最初のキリスト教布教開始。

Francis Xavier (Francisco de Javier) establishes Japan's first Christian
mission at Kagoshima.

1553   上杉謙信と武田信玄の第1回川中島の戦い。

First of the **Battles of Kawanakajima** between the warlords Uesugi
Kenshin and Takeda Shingen.

1559   大友宗麟、南蛮船(ポルトガル船が主)に豊後国の府内港を開く。

Ōtomo Sōrin opens the port of Funai in **Bungo Province** to *namban*
(Western) trade ships (mainly Portuguese ships).

1560   桶狭間の戦い：織田信長、今川義元を破る。

Battle of Okehazama: Oda Nobunaga defeats Imagawa Yoshimoto.

1563   イエズス会宣教師ルイス＝フロイス来日；後に「日本史」を著す。1549年か
ら1593年までの日本におけるイエズス会の布教の歴史と共に当時の日本に
関する記述も豊富。

Jesuit missionary Luis Frois arrives in Japan; he later writes
Historia de Japam, which covers the years 1549–93 and, though
chiefly a history of Jesuit activities, provides much information
about contemporary Japan.

雪舟「破墨山水図」
Sesshū Tōyō's Haboku Landscape

フランシスコ＝ザビエル
Francis Xavier

C＝コロンブス、バハマ諸島に上陸。
Christopher Columbus lands in the Bahamas. — **1492**

ヴァスコ＝ダ＝ガマ、喜望峰を廻ってインド、カリカットに到着。
Vasco da Gama, after a voyage around the Cape of Good Hope, reaches Calicut in India. — **1498**

マルチン＝ルター「95箇条の論題」をウィッテンベルグの教会のドアに張り出す。
Martin Luther nails the Ninety-Five Theses to the church door at Wittenberg. — **1517**

イグナティウス＝ロヨラ、イエズス会設立。
Founding of the Society of Jesus (Jesuits) by Ignatius of Loyola. — **1534**

ポルトガル、中国や日本と貿易するためマカオに中継地を確立。
Portuguese establish an entrepôt at Macao for trade with China and Japan. — **1557**

安土・桃山時代 Azuchi-Momoyama period (1568–1600)

安土桃山時代は織田信長、豊臣秀吉、徳川家康の3人の覇者の登場によって特徴づけられる。彼らは100年にわたる内乱を克服し、日本の政治的統一を成し遂げた。各地の武将は城を築き、狩野永徳に代表される豪華絢爛な文化が生まれた。この短い期間に日本はヨーロッパの貿易商や宣教師との接触を通じて南蛮文化にも触れた。

1568	織田信長、足利義昭を将軍に擁立して京都に入る。義昭、1573年に京都より追放される。
	Oda Nobunaga enters Kyōto, installs Ashikaga Yoshiaki as shōgun; Yoshiaki driven into exile in 1573.
1570	姉川の戦い：浅井長政、織田信長・徳川家康連合軍に敗退。
	Battle of Anegawa: Oda Nobunaga and Tokugawa Ieyasu defeat Asai Nagamasa.
1571	長崎に最初のポルトガル商船来航。
	First Portuguese merchant ship arrives to trade at Nagasaki.
	織田信長、比叡山延暦寺を焼き打ちする。
	Oda Nobunaga attacks and burns the temple Enryakuji on Mt. Hiei.
1575	長篠の戦い：織田信長、3,000人の鉄砲隊を配置して武田勝頼を破る。近代的戦法始まる。
	Battle of Nagashino: the 3,000 musketeers deployed by Oda Nobunaga in his victory over Takeda Katsuyori mark Japan's shift to modern warfare.
1576	信長安土城築城に着手。
	Oda Nobunaga begins construction of **Azuchi Castle**.
1579	イエズス会アジア地区の巡察師 A＝バリニャーノ来日。
	Alessandro Valignano, visitor (supervisor) of the **Jesuit** missions in Asia, arrives in Japan.
1580	要塞化した浄土真宗の石山本願寺織田信長に降伏。
	Oda Nobunaga captures the heavily fortified **Jōdo Shin sect** temple Ishiyama Honganji.
1582	天正遣欧使節：A＝バリニャーノの勧めにより4人のキリシタン少年をローマに派遣、法皇グレゴリ8世に謁見。
	Tenshō Embassy to Europe: four Christian Japanese boys are sent to Rome at the urging of Alessandro Valignano for an audience with Pope Gregory XIII.
	本能寺の変：覇者織田信長、家臣明智光秀の急襲を受け自害。
	Honnōji Incident: hegemon Oda Nobunaga commits suicide after a surprise attack by his vassal Akechi Mitsuhide.
	豊臣秀吉、山崎の戦いで光秀を破る。
	Toyotomi Hideyoshi defeats Mitsuhide in the **Battle of Yamazaki**.

The Azuchi-Momoyama period was defined by the rise of three successive hegemons, Oda Nobunaga, Toyotomi Hideyoshi, and Tokugawa Ieyasu, who brought about the political unification of Japan following a century of civil war. Warrior patronage supported the construction of castles throughout the country and a spectacular flourishing of the decorative arts, epitomized by the opulent style of artists such as Kanō Eitoku. During this brief period, Japan was also exposed to Western (*namban*) culture through contact with European traders and missionaries.

織田信長 **Oda Nobunaga**

イスパニア、マニラ市建設。
Spain founds Manila.

1571

安土城 **Azuchi Castle**

天正遣欧使節
Tenshō Embassy to Europe

秀吉太閤検地を開始、土地面積と収穫量を測量する。

Hideyoshi initiates the Taikō *kenchi*, a national survey of lands and their productive capacity.

1583　天下統一者豊臣秀吉、賤ヶ岳の戦いで柴田勝家を破る。

National unifier Toyotomi Hideyoshi defeats Shibata Katsuie in the **Battle of Shizugatake**.

豊臣秀吉、大坂城の築城開始。

Toyotomi Hideyoshi begins construction of Ōsaka Castle.

1587　禁教令：秀吉キリシタン宣教師全員の国外追放を布告。ただし布教は黙認。

Anti-Christian edicts: Toyotomi Hideyoshi issues an edict expelling all Christian missionaries from Japan; it is neither obeyed nor enforced.

豊臣秀吉北野天満宮で大茶会を催す。千利休・津田宗及らが亭主をつとめる。

Sen no Rikyū and Tsuda Sōgyū officiate at a grand outdoor tea ceremony held by Toyotomi Hideyoshi on the grounds of the **Kitano Shrine**.

1588　刀狩：秀吉、百姓の武器所有禁止の布告を出す。

Sword hunt: Toyotomi Hideyoshi issues an edict prohibiting possession of weapons by peasants.

1590　小田原征伐：秀吉後北条氏を滅ぼし天下統一を達成。

Odawara Campaign: Toyotomi Hideyoshi destroys the **Later Hōjō family**, pacifies all of Japan.

1592　文禄の役：秀吉、第1回朝鮮出兵。

Bunroku Campaign: first of Toyotomi Hideyoshi's invasions of Korea.

1596　サン・フェリペ号事件：豊臣秀吉、イスパニアの大型帆船サン・フェリペ号の船荷を没収する。カトリック宣教師の迫害を開始。

San Felipe **Incident**: Toyotomi Hideyoshi confiscates the Spanish galleon *San Felipe*, inaugurating his persecution of Catholic missionaries.

1597　26聖人殉教：豊臣秀吉、外国人を含む26人のキリシタンを長崎で磔にする。

Twenty-Six Martyrs: twenty-six Japanese and foreign Christians crucified at Nagasaki by order of Toyotomi Hideyoshi.

慶長の役：秀吉、第2回朝鮮出兵。

Keichō Campaign: second of Toyotomi Hideyoshi's invasions of Korea.

1598　豊臣秀吉、没する。

Toyotomi Hideyoshi dies.

慶長の役で朝鮮に出兵した秀吉の武将、陶工を携えて帰国する。彼らによって薩摩焼、有田焼、萩焼が生まれる。

Following the **second of the invasions of Korea in 1592 and 1597**, Toyotomi Hideyoshi's generals return to Japan with Korean potters who establish the traditions of **Satsuma ware**, **Arita ware**, and **Hagi ware**.

豊臣秀吉 **Toyotomi Hideyoshi**

スペインの無敵艦隊アルマダ、イギリス
艦隊に破れる。スペイン大西洋の制海権
を失う。
Spanish supremacy in the Atlantic
Ocean ends with the defeat of its
Invincible Armada by England.

1588

26聖人殉教 **Twenty-Six Martyrs**

江戸時代 Edo period (1600–1868)

関ヶ原の戦いの勝利によって徳川家康の全国にわたる覇権が確立し、江戸時代がはじまる。幕藩体制とよばれる政治体制を確立した徳川幕府の支配の下、2世紀を超える平和が続いた。しかしその間海外からの影響を避けるため鎖国政策をとって孤立した。町人の活気あふれるブルジョワ精神は歌舞伎や浄瑠璃を生み、戯作などの娯楽小説や浮世絵も発達した。1853年のペリー提督来航に続く激動の中で、幕府の国家最高機関としての機能は失われ、徳川体制は崩壊する。

1600	イギリス人水先案内人ウイリアム＝アダムズ(三浦按針)、オランダのリーフデ号に乗って日本に漂着。後に徳川家康に助言者として厚遇される。
	English pilot William Adams (Miura Anjin), who becomes a valued adviser to Tokugawa Ieyasu, arrives in Japan aboard the disabled Dutch vessel *Liefde*.
	関ヶ原の戦い：徳川家康、全土に覇権確立。
	Battle of Sekigahara: Tokugawa Ieyasu establishes hegemony over Japan.
1601	この頃徳川家康、豊臣秀吉が始めた**朱印船貿易**の許可証(朱印状)交付を始める。
	Around this time Tokugawa Ieyasu begins to issue licenses for the **vermilion seal ship trade**, which had been initiated by Toyotomi Hideyoshi.
1602	イスパニアの大型帆船エスピリツ＝サント号、嵐のため**土佐国**の清水港に漂着：ノバ＝イスパニア(メキシコ)との貿易を求める徳川家康は乗組員を釈放する。
	The Spanish galleon *Espiritu Santo*, blown off course in a storm, arrives in Shimizu Harbor in **Tosa Province**; Tokugawa Ieyasu, who seeks trade with New Spain (Mexico), releases the crew.
1603	徳川家康、**征夷大将軍**に任じられ**徳川幕府**はじまる。
	Tokugawa Ieyasu is granted the title of *seii tai shōgun* ("**barbarian-subduing generalissimo**"), founds the **Tokugawa shogunate**.
	出雲阿国、京都でかぶき踊りを演じ評判となる。これをもって歌舞伎の初めとする。
	Izumo no Okuni stages hugely successful dance dramas in Kyōto. This is generally regarded as the beginning of *kabuki*.
	イエズス会宣教師「日葡辞書」を編纂。
	Nippo jisho, a Japanese-Portuguese dictionary, is being compiled by Jesuit missionaries.

Victory in the Battle of Sekigahara established Tokugawa Ieyasu's hegemony over Japan, commencing the Edo period. Over two centuries of peace followed under the rule of the Tokugawa shogunate, which instituted a political structure known as the *bakuhan* system and isolated Japan from potentially disruptive foreign influences through its policy of National Seclusion (Sakoku). The vibrant bourgeois spirit of the period's thriving merchant class (*chōnin*) found expression in dramatic forms such as *kabuki* and *jōruri*, in the popular literature known as *gesaku*, and in artistic genres such as *ukiyo-e*. In the turbulent period following Commodore Matthew Perry's arrival in 1853, the shogunate lost its ability to assert national authority, and the Tokugawa regime collapsed.

徳川家康 **Tokugawa Ieyasu**

「豊臣秀吉朱印状」
Vermilion-Seal Trade License Issued by Toyotomi Hideyoshi

1600

勅許状によってイギリス東インド会社を設立。
British East India Company incorporated by royal charter.

1602

オランダ政府、オランダ東インド会社に東インド貿易の独占権を与える。
Dutch government grants the Dutch East India Company a monopoly on trade in the East Indies.

1604

イエズス会宣教師 J＝ロドリゲスがポルトガル語で書いた日本語の発音と文法の入門書「日本大文典」(1604年〜1608年)の出版はじまる。

Jesuit missionary João Rodrigues begins publication of *Arte da Lingoa de Iapam* (1604–08), a comprehensive introduction in Portuguese to written and spoken Japanese.

1607

朝鮮李朝(1392年〜1910年)から徳川幕府へ最初の朝鮮通信使、江戸に到着。

Arrival in Edo of the first Chōsen *tsūshinshi*, a series of embassies from **Yi dynasty** (1392–1910) Korea to the Tokugawa shogunate.

1609

薩摩藩主島津氏、幕府の許可を得て琉球諸島に武力侵攻；琉球は1611年薩摩藩に従属する。

With the approval of the shogunate, the **Shimazu family**, lords of the **Satsuma domain**, mount a military expedition against the Ryūkyū Islands; the Ryūkyūs become a vassal state of Satsuma in 1611.

平戸にオランダ商館をおく；オランダ貿易はじまる。

Dutch Factory established at Hirado; **Dutch trade** begins.

マードレ・デ・デウス号事件：徳川家康、ポルトガル船マードレ・デ・デウス号船長の逮捕を命じる；翌年、船長は船の引き渡しを拒みみずから爆沈。

Madre de Deus **Incident**: Tokugawa Ieyasu orders the arrest of the captain of the Portuguese ship *Madre de Deus*; the following year the captain destroys his ship rather than surrender.

1610

京都の商人田中勝助、徳川家康の許可を得て R＝ビベロ＝イ＝ベラスコの帰国に同行、ノバ＝イスパニア(メキシコ)に渡る。

Kyōto merchant Tanaka Shōsuke receives permission from Tokugawa Ieyasu to accompany Rodrigo Vivero y Velasco on his return to New Spain (Mexico).

1611

ノバ＝イスパニア(メキシコ)総督の使節 S＝ビスカイノ、引退した徳川家康と現将軍徳川秀忠への謁見を許される。

Sebastian Viscaino, envoy of the viceroy of New Spain (Mexico), is granted an audience with the retired shōgun Tokugawa Ieyasu and the shōgun Tokugawa Hidetada.

1612

禁教令：幕府キリスト教を禁じる。

Anti-Christian edicts: shogunate issues directives aimed at restricting Christianity.

1613

J＝セーリス、イギリス国王ジェームス1世の国書を持って来日；徳川家康に謁見して、イギリスの通商許可を得る。

John Saris arrives in Japan with credentials from King James I of England; he petitions Tokugawa Ieyasu and receives permission for the English to trade.

仙台藩主伊達政宗、支倉常長率いる使節をスペインに派遣。フイリップ3世にノバ＝イスパニア(メキシコ)との通商を求めたが失敗。

Date Masamune, *daimyō* of Sendai, dispatches an embassy led by Hasekura Tsunenaga to Spain to petition Philip III (unsuccessfully) for the establishment of trade relations with New Spain (Mexico).

1614

キリスト教禁教令、全国に広がる。

Ban on Christianity extended nationwide.

最初の大坂城包囲始まる。(大坂冬の陣)

First of the Sieges of Ōsaka Castle begins.

北米大陸バージニア州にイギリス植民地 **1607**
ジェームズタウン建設。
English settlement established in
North America at Jamestown,
Virginia.

J＝ケプラー、「新天文学」の中で彼の惑星 **1609**
運動3法則のうち第1、第2法則を発表。
Johannes Kepler publishes the first
two of his three laws of planetary
motion in *Astronomia Nova*.

朝鮮通信使
Embassies from Yi Dynasty

支倉常長 **Hasekura Tsunenaga**

1615

第2回大坂城包囲(大坂夏の陣)；豊臣秀吉の息子で跡継ぎの豊臣秀頼、自害。

Second of the Sieges of Ōsaka Castle; Toyotomi Hideyoshi's son and appointed heir Toyotomi Hideyori commits suicide.

幕府は、領内の城を一つに制限する一国一城令、**武家諸法度、禁中並公家諸法度**を公布する。

Shogunate issues an order limiting castles to one per domain (the Ikkoku Ichijō Rei), promulgates the Buke Shohatto (**Laws for the Military Houses**) and Kinchū narabi ni Kuge Shohatto (**Laws Governing the Imperial Court and Nobility**).

1616

徳川家康、没する。

Tokugawa Ieyasu dies.

外国船寄港地を長崎と平戸に制限する。

European shipping limited to the ports of Nagasaki and Hirado.

1624

平戸の**イギリス商館**、経営不振のため閉鎖。商館長 R＝コックスの日記は、当時の平戸の様子をよく伝える。

English Factory in Hirado closes due to poor business. The diary of Richard Cocks, manager of the factory, is a rich source of information about daily life in Hirado.

イスパニア船の来航を禁止；キリシタン迫害を強化する。

Spanish ships prohibited from calling at Japanese ports; persecution of Christians intensifies.

1635

徳川将軍、大君の称号を用いる。

Tokugawa shōguns adopt the title of *taikun*.

外国船の寄港地を長崎に限定(ただし**オランダ商館**は平戸で活動を続ける)；**海外渡航禁止令**公布(日本人の海外渡航と海外に居住する日本人の帰国をいっさい禁止)；新造船は500石(49トン)に制限。

All foreign shipping restricted to the port of Nagasaki (nonetheless, the **Dutch Factory** remains active in Hirado); **Prohibitions of Foreign Voyages** instituted (overseas travel by Japanese is prohibited, and Japanese residents abroad are prohibited from returning to Japan); capacity of newly constructed ships limited to 500 *koku* (49 gross tons).

武家諸法度改定；大名の参勤交代制度化される。

Revision of the Buke Shohatto (**Laws for the Military Houses**); system of mandatory alternate residence in Edo by *daimyō* (the *sankin kōtai* system) formalized.

1636

長崎に人工島出島完成：1571年以来市中にあったポルトガル商人の居住地を出島に制限。

Buildings on the artificial island of Dejima at Nagasaki completed; Portuguese merchants, who since 1571 had lived freely in the city, are removed there.

1637

島原の乱(1637年～1638年)、重い年貢に苦しむ農民が蜂起。

Shimabara Uprising (1637–38) mounted by overtaxed peasants.

1639

鎖国の諸法令完成：オランダ人を除く全ヨーロッパ人の来航禁止。

Edicts establishing **National Seclusion** (Sakoku) are completed: Portuguese merchants are evicted from Dejima; Portuguese ships are banned from Japan; all Westerners except the Dutch are prohibited from entering Japan.

踏絵 **Fumie**

W = シェークスピア、没する。 **1616**
William Shakespeare dies.

ジャワのバタビアにオランダ商館設立; **1619**
オランダ東インド会社の根拠地となる。
Dutch Factory established at Batavia
in Java; it becomes the headquarters
of the Dutch East India Company.

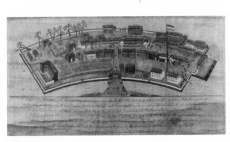

出島 **Dejima**

1641   オランダ商館、長崎の平戸から出島に移される。

Dutch Factory shifted from Hirado to Dejima in Nagasaki.

1643   徳川幕府、農地の売買を禁止する田畑永代売買禁止令公布。

Tahata (or Dempata) Eitai Baibai Kinshi Rei, an ordinance
prohibiting the sale and purchase of farmland, issued by the
Tokugawa shogunate.

1651   慶安事件：由井正雪、倒幕を企てるが失敗に終わる。

Keian Incident: Yui Shōsetsu plots a coup d'état unsuccessfully
against the Tokugawa shogunate.

この頃、江戸で浪人が増える；旗本奴・町奴と呼ばれる無頼の集団が治安
を乱す。

Around this time the population of *rōnin* (**masterless** *samurai*) in
Edo swells; bands of ruffians called *hatamoto yakko* and *machi yakko*
create problems of public order.

1657   明暦の大火江戸を焼きつくし死者10万人以上に及ぶ。江戸城の大半と寺社
350以上が焼失。

Meireki Fire ravages Edo, killing more than 100,000 people; much of
Edo Castle and more than 350 shrines and temples burn.

徳川光圀の命により「大日本史」の編集始まる(1906年完成)。

Compilation of the national history *Dai Nihon shi* (**History of Great
Japan**) begins at the behest of Tokugawa Mitsukuni (it is completed
in 1906).

1665   宗門改：徳川幕府禁教のため諸藩に定期的信仰調査を命令。

Shūmon aratame (**religious inquisition**): **Tokugawa shogunate**
orders *daimyō* to conduct a yearly inquisition of religion to eradicate
Christianity.

1682   井原西鶴の好色冒険物語「好色一代男」刊行。

Ihara Saikaku publishes the amorous adventure tale *Kōshoku ichidai
otoko* (tr *The Life of an Amorous Man*).

1685   将軍徳川綱吉、最初の生類憐みの令を公布。

First of the Shōrui Awaremi no Rei (**Edicts on Compassion for
Living Things**) issued by the shōgun Tokugawa Tsunayoshi.

1688   元禄時代(1688年～1704年)はじまる。歌舞伎、浄瑠璃の黄金時代として知
られる文化の開花期。

Beginning of the **Genroku era** (1688–1704), a time of cultural
flowering known in particular as the golden age of *kabuki* and *jōruri*
(the puppet drama).

柳沢吉保、将軍徳川綱吉の側用人に任命される。

Yanagisawa Yoshiyasu appointed *sobayōnin* (**grand chamberlain**) to
the shōgun Tokugawa Tsunayoshi.

1689   松尾芭蕉「奥の細道」の旅に出立。

Matsuo Bashō departs on the journey through northern Honshū that
he later chronicles in the *haiku* travel diary *Oku no hosomichi* (tr *The
Narrow Road of the Deep North*).

オランダ、ポルトガルからマラッカを攻 **1641**
め取る。
Dutch capture Malacca from the
Portuguese.

中国に満州族による清王朝(1644年〜 **1644**
1912年)成立。
Manchus establish the Qing dynasty
(1644–1912) in China.

明暦の大火 **Meireki Fire**

井原西鶴 **Ihara Saikaku**

イギリス「権利の宣言」制定；議会の同 **1689**
意のない課税禁止される。
English Bill of Rights enacted; the
levying of taxes requires the consent
of Parliament.

1690

ドイツ人医師 E＝ケンペル、長崎のオランダ商館に到着；著書「日本誌」
(全2巻)は1727年英語で出版され、19世紀までヨーロッパの日本研究の古
典とされた。

German physician Engelbert Kaempfer arrives at Nagasaki to serve
at the Dutch Factory; his two-volume *History of Japan*, first
published in English in 1727, is the standard European work on
Japan until the 19th century.

1703

赤穂事件：赤穂藩浪士大石良雄ら仇敵吉良義央を討つ(元禄15年12月15日)。
Forty-Seven Rōnin Incident (31 January 1703): band of former
retainers of the **Akō domain**, under the leadership of Ōishi Yoshio,
carry out a vendetta against Kira Yoshinaka.

近松門左衛門の浄瑠璃「曾根崎心中」上演される。後に歌舞伎でも上演。

First performance of *Sonezaki shinjū* (tr *The Love Suicides at
Sonezaki*), Chikamatsu Monzaemon's *jōruri* drama (later a *kabuki*
drama) about a love suicide.

1707

富士山噴火。

Last eruption of Mt. Fuji (as of 1999).

1708

イエズス会宣教師 G＝B＝シドッチ日本に上陸するがただちにとらえられ
る。江戸に送られ、新井白石の尋問を受ける。

Jesuit missionary Giovanni Battista Sidotti arrives in Japan but is
arrested immediately; he is transported to Edo and interrogated by
Arai Hakuseki.

1709

新井白石、将軍を補佐し正徳の治(1709年～1716年)として知られる一連の
改革を始める。

Arai Hakuseki becomes a key shogunal adviser; commencement of
the series of reforms known as the Shōtoku no Chi (1709–16).

1715

正徳長崎新例(令)：長崎における中国とオランダの貿易を制限する諸令を
公布；年間の貿易船の数を、中国船は30艘、オランダ船は2艘に制限。

Shōtoku Nagasaki Shinrei: New regulations issued restricting
foreign trade with the Chinese and Dutch at Nagasaki; Chinese
limited to 30 and Dutch to 2 trade ships annually.

新井白石、西洋の社会事情や地理などの研究書「西洋紀聞」の草稿を完成。

Shogunal adviser Arai Hakuseki completes the first draft of his
study of Western society and geography, *Seiyō kibun* (**Tidings of the
West**).

1716

徳川吉宗将軍となる；享保の改革(1716年～1745年)はじまる。

Tokugawa Yoshimune becomes shōgun; **Kyōhō Reforms** (1716–45)
commence.

1718

江戸に**町火消**(町人の消防組織)設置。

Fire brigades of townsmen (*machi hikeshi*) formed in Edo.

1721

将軍徳川吉宗、民意を聞くため**目安箱**を設置。

Meyasubako (**a suggestion box**) is posted to receive commoner
appeals to the shōgun.

1723

心中流行し、幕府は防止策を講じる。

Rash of **love suicides** (*shinjū*) leads to government attempts to
discourage them.

イングランド銀行創立。
Bank of England incorporated.

1694

中国、イギリスに広東での貿易を許可する。
Chinese permit the English to conduct annual trade operations at Guangzhou.

1699

近松門左衛門
Chikamatsu Monzaemon

ピョートル大帝、サンクト＝ペテルブルグを建設し、西への海の出口を得る。
Tsar Peter I of Russia founds St. Petersburg and gains a sea outlet to the West.

1703

T＝ニューコメン、イギリスのスタッフォードシャーにおいて鉱山から排水するための蒸気機関を設置。
Thomas Newcomen erects a steam engine to pump water from a mine in Staffordshire, England.

1712

徳川吉宗 **Tokugawa Yoshimune**

1732 　西南日本にイナゴと天候不順による**享保の飢饉**おこる。

Locust plague and unseasonable weather cause **Kyōhō Famine** in southwestern Japan.

1736 　銅輸出を抑制するため、中国船の入港を年間25艘に制限。

Chinese trade ships limited to 25 vessels annually to reduce the flow of copper out of Japan.

1748 　赤穂事件(1703年)を主題にした浄瑠璃「**仮名手本忠臣蔵**」が初演される。後に歌舞伎で上演。

First performance of the *jōruri* drama (later a *kabuki* drama) *Kanadehon chūshingura* (tr *Chūshingura: The Treasury of Loyal Retainers*), a historical work based on the **Forty-Seven Rōnin Incident** of 1703.

1767 　田沼意次、**側用人**となり商業を振興して幕府の収入増を図る；1786年失脚。

Tanuma Okitsugu becomes *sobayōnin* (**grand chamberlain**) and attempts to increase shogunal income through the expansion of commerce; he falls from power in 1786.

この頃、**百姓一揆**(農民の反乱)と**打毀**(都市の暴動)の発生が次第に増加。

Around this time, **peasant uprisings** (*hyakushō ikki*) and **urban riots** (*uchikowashi*) occur with increasing frequency.

1774 　杉田玄白、前野良沢らわが国初の西洋医学書の翻訳「**解体新書**」刊行。

Anatomical text *Kaitai shinsho* (**New Book of Anatomy**) published by Sugita Gempaku and Maeno Ryōtaku; it is the first complete Japanese translation of a Western medical work.

1776 　上田秋成、怪異小説「**雨月物語**」を出版。

Ueda Akinari publishes *Ugetsu monogatari* (tr *Tales of Moonlight and Rain*), a collection of supernatural tales.

1782 　**天明の飢饉**はじまる；飢饉の5年間に死者は全国で20万人から90万人におよんだといわれる。

Temmei Famine begins; estimates of the nationwide death toll during the five years of its duration range from 200,000 to 900,000.

1783 　浅間山噴火し約2万人の死者を出す；降灰による冷夏と農作物の不作のため前年に始まった飢饉が悪化する。

Asamayama erupts, causing some 20,000 deaths; falling ash brings low summer temperatures and poor crops, exacerbating the famine that had commenced the previous year.

1787 　松平定信**老中**となる；寛政の改革(1787年～1793年)始まる。

Matsudaira Sadanobu becomes **senior shogunal councillor** (*rōjū*); **Kansei Reforms** (1787–93) initiated.

1789 　旗本・御家人の窮乏を救うため、**棄捐令**(借金支払い猶予令)公布。

Debt moratoriums (*kienrei*) declared to save shogunal retainers from destitution.

1790 　浮世絵画家喜多川歌麿、この頃代表作となる女性の半身像**大首絵**を描く。

Ukiyo-e artist Kitagawa Utamaro begins producing *ōkubi-e* (**bust portraits**), his most distinctive and memorable designs of women.

1791 　幕府、江戸市中の銭湯の男女混浴を禁止。

Shogunate prohibits communal bathing of men and women at **public bathhouses** in Edo.

田沼意次 **Tanuma Okitsugu**

D=デイドロ、「百科全書」(全35巻)の出版を始める。
Denis Diderot begins publication of the 35-volume *Encyclopédie*. **1751**

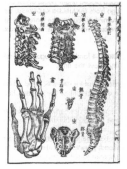

「解体新書」 **Kaitai Shinsho**

アメリカ、大陸会議でアメリカ独立宣言発布。
Continental Congress issues the US Declaration of Independence. **1776**

E=カートライト、力織機を発明。
Edmund Cartwright patents a power loom. **1785**

ジョージ=ワシントン、アメリカ合衆国初代大統領に就任。
George Washington becomes the first president of the United States. **1789**
フランス革命はじまる。
French Revolution begins.

1792

林子平、蟄居を命じられる：幕府は、外国の江戸湾侵入の可能性を論じた著書「海国兵談」(1791年)の板木・製本ともに没収。

Hayashi Shihei placed under house arrest; the shogunate confiscates the printing blocks and all copies of his book *Kaikoku heidan* (1791; **Discussion of the Military Problems of a Maritime Nation**), in which he discusses the possibility of foreign incursions into Edo Bay.

Ａ＝Ｅ＝ラクスマン、大黒屋光太夫を伴って蝦夷地東部の根室に来航；翌年日露の通商関係樹立を松前の幕吏と交渉するが、不調に終る。

Adam Erikovich Laxman arrives at Nemuro in eastern Ezochi (now Hokkaidō) with Daikokuya Kōdayū; the following year Laxman negotiates unsuccessfully with shogunal officials in Matsumae for the establishment of trade relations between Japan and Russia.

1796

稲村三伯ら、蘭日辞典「波留麻和解」を刊行。

Inamura Sampaku and others publish the Dutch-Japanese dictionary *Haruma wage* (**Halma Translated**).

1798

本居宣長「古事記」の注釈書「古事記伝」完成；国学の代表的研究書。

Motoori Norinaga completes the *Kojiki den*, a comprehensive annotation of the early historical narrative *Kojiki* (**Record of Ancient Matters**) and a major work in the Kokugaku (**National Learning**) movement.

近藤重蔵、千島列島を探検。

Kondō Jūzō explores the **Kuril Islands**.

1799

高田屋嘉兵衛、択捉航路を開拓。幕府、**箱館奉行**を設置。蝦夷地南部を直接行政支配。

Takataya Kahei establishes a shipping route to Etorofu. Shogunate establishes the Hakodate *bugyō* (**commissioner of Hakodate**) and controls over the southern part of Ezochi.

1800

伊能忠敬、日本地図作成のため全国の測量はじめる：1816年完了。

Inō Tadataka begins his cartographic survey of all Japan; it is completed in 1816.

1802

十返舎一九の滑稽本「東海道中膝栗毛」初編刊行；弥次郎兵と喜多八の江戸から大坂までの道中記。

Jippensha Ikku publishes the first volume of his serial comic novel *Tōkaidōchū hizakurige* (tr *Shank's Mare*), which describes the adventures of two wayfarers, Yajirobei and Kitahachi, on the road from Edo to Ōsaka.

1804

ロシア使節Ｎ＝Ｐ＝レザノフ長崎に来航。通商を要求したが容れられず。

Russian envoy Nikolai Petrovich Rezanov reaches Nagasaki, unsuccessfully seeks the establishment of trade relations with Japan.

1807

曲亭(滝沢)馬琴、為朝の武勇伝「椿説弓張月」の出版はじまる。

Kyokutei (Takizawa) Bakin begins publication of the adventure tale *Chinsetsu yumiharizuki* (**Crescent Moon: The Adventures of Tametomo**).

本居宣長 **Motoori Norinaga**

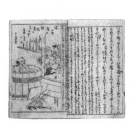

「東海道中膝栗毛」 **Shank's Mare**

エドワード=ジェンナー、初の天然痘予防接種に成功。
Edward Jenner performs first smallpox inoculation.

1796

フランスでメートル法、制定される。
Metric system instituted in France.

1799

ナポレオン、フランス皇帝となる。
Napoleon crowns himself emperor of France.

1804

R=フルトン、アメリカ合衆国ハドソン川で蒸気船の運行を始める。
Robert Fulton initiates steamboat service on the Hudson River.

1807

1808　フェートン号事件：イギリス軍艦フェートン号、オランダ旗を掲げて長崎港に侵入。オランダ商館員2名を捕らえ、食料と水を要求する；幕府、異国侵入の不安を募らす。

Phaeton Incident: British warship *Phaeton* enters Nagasaki Harbor under a Dutch flag, takes two Dutch traders who are released in exchange for food and water; the incident exacerbates shogunal fears of encroachment from the West.

1809　間宮林蔵、タタール海峡(間宮海峡)を発見。樺太が島であることを確認。

Mamiya Rinzō discovers the **Tatar Strait**, proving that **Sakhalin** is an island.

1811　ロシア軍艦ディアーナ号艦長Ｖ＝Ｍ＝ゴローニン、千島列島調査中に幕府にとらえられ投獄される(1813年釈放)。体験記「日本幽囚記」(1816年)は1818年に英訳され、広く読まれた。

Vasilii Mikhailovich Golovnin, captain of the Russian naval vessel *Diana*, is captured and imprisoned by the Japanese while surveying the **Kuril Islands** (he is released in 1813). His account of his experiences, published in 1816, is translated into English in 1818 as *Narrative of My Captivity in Japan, during the Years 1811, 1812, and 1813* and is widely read.

1812　高田屋嘉兵衛、千島列島国後沖でロシア軍艦に捕まる；1813年に帰還し、Ｖ＝Ｍ＝ゴローニンの釈放に努力する。

Takataya Kahei is taken captive by a Russian warship off Kunashiri in the **Kuril Islands**; freed in 1813, he negotiates the release of Vasilii Mikhailovich Golovnin.

1814　黒住宗忠、黒住教を開く。

Kurozumi Munetada founds the religious sect Kurozumikyō.

1820　小林一茶句文集「おらが春」完成。愛娘さとに対する愛情とその死に対する悲嘆がテーマ。

Kobayashi Issa completes the poetical diary *Oraga haru* (tr *The Year of My Life*); its theme is the author's love for his infant daughter Sato and the grief aroused by her sudden death.

1823　シーボルト、オランダ商館医師として来日；翌年鳴滝塾を開き、高野長英、伊東玄朴、伊藤圭介らにヨーロッパの医学や科学を教える。

Philipp Franz von Siebold arrives in Japan to serve as physician to the **Dutch Factory**; the following year he opens the boarding school Narutakijuku and teaches Western medicine and science to Takano Chōei, Itō Gemboku, and Itō Keisuke.

1825　幕府、異国船打払令を発布。

Shogunate issues the Ikokusen Uchiharai Rei (**Order for the Repelling of Foreign Ships**).

1829　Ｐ＝Ｆ＝シーボルト、高橋景保から日本地図を入手した罪で出島に自宅監禁となり、その後国外追放の処分をうける；オランダに帰国後、日本に関する博物学的研究「日本」「日本動物誌」「日本植物誌」を著す。

Physician Philipp Franz von Siebold placed under house arrest at Dejima for receiving maps of the Japanese archipelago from Takahashi Kageyasu. Siebold is subsequently banished from Japan; after returning to the Netherlands he writes the encyclopedic study

間宮林蔵 **Mamiya Rinzō**

イギリス、シンガポールを建設。
British found Singapore.

1819

アメリカ合衆国大統領 J = モンロー、モンロー主義宣言を発表。
US president James Monroe proclaims the Monroe Doctrine.

1823

シーボルト, P=F
Philipp Franz von Siebolt

of Japan, *Nippon, Archiv zur Beschreibung von Japan*, as well as *Fauna Japonica* and *Flora Japonica*.

1831　この頃、葛飾北斎の浮世絵風景画シリーズ「富嶽三十六景」の刊行始まる。

Katsushika Hokusai's series of *ukiyo-e* landscapes *Fugaku sanjūrokkei* (**Thirty-Six Views of Mt. Fuji**) begins to appear by about this time.

1832　為永春水、代表的人情本の恋愛小説「春色梅児誉美」の出版を始める。

Tamenaga Shunsui begins publication of the romantic novel *Shunshoku umegoyomi* (**Spring Love: A Plum Blossom Almanac**). It becomes the prototype of the *ninjōbon* ("**books about human feelings**").

1833　天保の飢饉(1833年〜1836年)はじまる；米の収穫は通常の1/3に減り、餓死・疫病死した者は20〜30万人におよぶ。

Tempō Famine (1833–36) begins; by 1836 rice harvests are estimated to have been only one-third of the normal crop; some 200,000 to 300,000 people are thought to have died of starvation and disease.

安藤広重の浮世絵風景画シリーズ「東海道五十三次」の刊行始まる。

Pubication of Andō Hiroshige's *ukiyo-e* landscape series *Tōkaidō gojūsantsugi* (**Fifty-Three Stations of the Tōkaidō Road**) begins.

1837　儒学者大塩平八郎の乱；農民を飢饉から救うため兵をおこす。

Rebellion of Ōshio Heihachirō, a Confucian ideologue who seeks famine relief for the peasantry.

生田万の乱；飢える農民を救おうとする。

Rebellion of Ikuta Yorozu, who seeks relief for starving farmers.

モリソン号事件：日本人漂流民を乗せたアメリカ商船モリソン号、江戸に近い浦賀、続いて九州の鹿児島湾に入港しようとして砲撃される。

Morrison Incident: US merchant ship carrying Japanese castaways is fired on as it attempts to enter Uraga Bay near Edo (now Tōkyō) and then Kagoshima Bay in Kyūshū.

1838　中山みき、天理教を開く。

Nakayama Miki founds the religious sect Tenrikyō.

1839　蛮社の獄：幕府、洋学者を弾圧。

Bansha no Goku (**Imprisonment of the Companions of Barbarian Studies**): shogunate crackdown on scholars of **Western Learning**.

1841　老中水野忠邦、天保の改革(1841年〜1843年)を開始。

Tempō Reforms (1841–43) initiated by senior shogunal councillor Mizuno Tadakuni.

漁師中浜万次郎(ジョン万次郎)、鳥島に漂着。アメリカの捕鯨船に救助されアメリカへ伴われる。

Fisherman Nakahama Manjirō (also known as John Manjirō), shipwrecked on the island of Torishima, is rescued by an American whaler and taken to the United States.

1842　異国船打払令、解除される：幕府、外国船に対して食料、水、薪を与えるよう命令。(新水供与令)

Ikokusen Uchiharai Rei (**Order for the Repelling of Foreign Ships**) revoked; shogunate orders the provision of food, water, and firewood to foreign ships (Shinsui Kyōyo Rei).

M＝ファラデイ、発電機を発明。   **1831**
Michael Faraday invents the dynamo.

広重「東海道五十三次」
**Hiroshige's Fifty-Three Stations
of the Tōkaidō Road**

イギリスヴィクトリア女王即位(1837年   **1837**
～1901年)。
Victoria becomes queen of England
(1837–1901).

水野忠邦 **Mizuno Tadakuni**

中国でアヘン戦争(1839年～1842年)はじ   **1839**
まる。
Opium War begins in China (1839–
42).

中浜万次郎 **Nakahama Manjirō**

1843   人返し：江戸に流れこんだ農民に帰村を命令する。

Hitogaeshi: peasants in Edo ordered to return to their farmlands.

上知令(土地接収の命令)、天保の改革の一つとして発布；江戸・大坂周辺
の土地の天領への編入をこころみるが、すぐに廃止される；水野忠邦失脚。

Agechirei (**Land Requisition Orders**) issued as part of the **Tempō
Reforms** but soon rescinded; this ordinance designated all lands
around Edo and Ōsaka as *tenryō* (**land under direct shogunal
control**); fall of Mizuno Tadakuni.

1844   オランダ国王の開国勧告書を持って、オランダ軍艦が長崎に到着；翌年、
幕府は文書で拒絶する。

Dutch warship arrives in Nagasaki with a letter from the king of the
Netherlands advising the shogunate to open Japan to trade with the
West; the following year the shogunate sends a letter of refusal.

蝦夷地の箱館に守備隊と砲台置かれる；千島列島の国後に守備隊置かれる。

Garrison and battery established at Hakodate in Ezochi; garrison
established on Kunashiri in the **Kuril Islands**.

1846   外国の軍艦と捕鯨船、日本沿海への来航増える；幕府および諸藩は沿岸警
備を強化する。

Foreign warships and **whaling vessels** enter Japanese waters with
increasing frequency; the shogunate and a number of domains give
greater attention to coastal defenses.

1852   オランダ商館最後の館長 J＝H＝ドンケル＝クルチウス来日。

Jan Hendrik Donker Curtius, the last overseer of the **Dutch Factory**,
arrives in Japan.

1853   ペリー提督、アメリカ東インド艦隊の4艦を率い江戸湾口の浦賀に投錨。

Four warships of the US East India Squadron, commanded by
Commodore Matthew Perry, call at Uraga at the mouth of Edo Bay.

ロシアの副元帥 E＝V＝プチャーチン、旗艦パルラダと4隻の軍艦を率いて
長崎に来航。

Russian Vice Admiral Evfimii Vasil'evich Putiatin calls at Nagasaki
with the flagship *Pallada* and four other warships.

1854   ペリー提督、7艦を率いて江戸湾に停泊。

Fleet of seven US naval vessels, led by Commodore Matthew Perry,
anchors in Edo Bay.

日米和親条約(神奈川条約)調印；ついで英国(1854年)、ロシア(1855年)、オ
ランダ(1856年)とも和親条約を結ぶ。

**Treaty of Peace and Amity between the United States and the
Empire of Japan** (**Kanagawa Treaty**) signed; similar treaties
concluded with Great Britain (1854), Russia (1855), and the
Netherlands (1856).

1855   安政大地震；江戸で7000人以上の死者。

Ansei Earthquake; more than 7,000 die in Edo.

海軍伝習所(海軍士官の訓練校)、長崎に設立。

Kaigun Denshūjo (**naval-officer training school**) established at
Nagasaki.

1856   洋学研究および洋書翻訳のため蕃書調所設立。

Bansho Shirabesho (**Institute for the Investigation of Barbarian**

ワシントンとボルチイモアの間に電信装 **1844**
置つながる。
Telegraph line links Washington and
Baltimore.

イギリスのロイター通信社、設立。 **1851**
British news agency Reuters founded.

ペリー提督
Commodore Matthew Perry

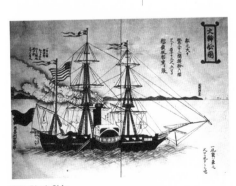

黒船 **Black Ship**

Books) is established for the translation of Western languages and the study of the West.

駐日アメリカ総領事ハリスが下田に着任。幕府と**ハリス条約**(**日米修好通商条約**)の交渉開始。

US consul general Townsend Harris arrives at Shimoda to initiate negotiations with the shogunate on what will become the **Harris Treaty (United States-Japan Treaty of Amity and Commerce)**.

吉田松陰松下村塾を開き長州藩の若い武士に**尊皇論**を教え始める。

Yoshida Shōin establishes Shōka Sonjuku and begins to teach his **imperial loyalist philosophy** to young *samurai* of the Chōshū domain.

1857 鉄生産のための**反射炉**、伊豆半島の韮山に完成。

Hansharo (**reverberatory furnace**) for the production of steel completed at Nirayama on the Izu Peninsula.

1858 井伊直弼、**大老**となる。

Ii Naosuke becomes **senior adviser to the shōgun** (*tairō*).

幕府、**安政5ヵ国条約**をアメリカ合衆国、オランダ、ロシア、イギリス、フランスと締結。

Ansei commercial treaties are concluded between the shogunate and the United States, the Netherlands, Russia, Great Britain, and France.

幕府の開国に反対する者に対し、**安政の大獄**(1858年〜1860年)始まる。

Beginning of the **Ansei Purge** (1858–60) of opponents to the shogunate's opening of Japan to the West.

1859 イギリス領事R＝オールコック将軍、来日；幕府との交渉記録「**大君の都**」を1863年に出版。

British consul general Rutherford Alcock arrives in Japan; *The Capital of the Tycoon*, his account of his dealings with the shogunate, is published in 1863.

イギリス商人T＝B＝グラバー、来日；グラバー商会は、倒幕活動の中心である薩摩藩と長州藩に武器を供給する。

British merchant Thomas Blake Glover arrives in Japan; Glover and Co. supplies arms to the domains of Satsuma and Chōshū, centers of antishogunal activity.

J＝C＝ヘボン来日；わが国初の和英辞典「**和英語林集成**」(1867年)を完成。

James Curtis Hepburn arrives in Japan; his *Japanese and English Dictionary* (1867; J; *Waei gorin shūsei*) is the first Japanese-English dictionary.

川手文治郎金光教を開く。

Kawate Bunjirō founds the religious sect Konkōkyō.

1860 万延元年遣米使節、ハリス条約批准のためアメリカ軍艦ポーハタン号でアメリカに向けて出発。咸臨丸(艦長勝海舟)同行。

Shogunal mission to the United States leaves aboard the American warship *Powhatan* to ratify the Harris Treaty. It is accompanied by the *Kanrin maru*, with a Japanese crew under the command of Katsu Kaishū.

ハリス, T Townsend Harris

反射炉 Reverberatory Furnace

中国、英・仏・露・米と天津条約を結ぶ。 **1858**
China signs Treaties of Tianjin with
Great Britain, France, Russia, and the
United States.
インド政府、条例で正式にインド統治権
をイギリス王に譲る。
Government of India Act formally
transfers control over India to British
crown.

フランス軍サイゴンを占領。 **1859**
French forces occupy Saigon.
スエズ運河の建設始まる；1869年完成。
Construction of the Suez Canal
begins; completed in 1869.
C=ダーウイン「種の起源」を出版。
Charles Darwin publishes *On the
Origin of Species*.

咸臨丸 Kanrin Maru

桜田門外の変：井伊直弼暗殺される。

Sakuradamongai Incident: assassination of Ii Naosuke.

この頃から大量の浮世絵がヨーロッパに輸出される；フランスにジャポニズムおこる。

From about this time large quantities of *ukiyo-e* prints are exported to Europe; *Japonisme* appears in France.

1861

日本で最初の近代的新聞「ナガサキ＝シッピング＝リスト＝アンド＝アドバタイザー」(長崎の船舶一覧と広告)の発行が英語で始まる。

Publication of the *Nagasaki Shipping List and Advertiser*, Japan's first modern newspaper, begins; it is in English.

1862

初の定期的日本語新聞「官板バタビヤ新聞」の発行始まる；バタビヤ(ジャカルタ)のオランダ総督府機関誌「ジャワシェ＝クーラント」を蕃書調所で翻訳。

First regularly published Japanese-language newspaper, *Kampan Batabiya shimbun*, translated at the Bansho Shirabesho from a Dutch colony publication in Batavia, the *Javasche Courant*, begins publication.

坂下門外の変：老中筆頭安藤信正襲撃される。孝明天皇の妹、和宮皇女と将軍徳川家茂の結婚に反対してくわだてられる。婚儀は同年おこなわれる。

Sakashitamongai Incident: assassination attempt on Andō Nobumasa, leading **senior councillor** (*rōjū*) of the shogunate. The incident is a reaction to the planned marriage of the shōgun Tokugawa Iemochi to Princess Kazu, sister of Emperor Kōmei. The marriage in fact takes place later this year.

リチャードソン事件(生麦事件)：薩摩藩士、イギリス商人リチャードソンを殺害。

Richardson Affair (**Namamugi Incident**): murder of a British merchant by retainers of the Satsuma domain.

幕府初の海外留学生、西周と津田真道をオランダに派遣。

Nishi Amane and Tsuda Mamichi, the first students dispatched overseas by the shogunate, depart for the Netherlands.

最初の英和辞典「英和対訳袖珍辞書」出版。

Publication of the first English-Japanese dictionary, *Eiwa taiyaku shūchin jisho*.

1863

薩英戦争：生麦事件の報復として、イギリスの軍艦薩摩藩を攻撃。

Kagoshima Bombardment: British warships attack the Satsuma domain in retaliation for the Richardson Affair.

文久3年8月18日(1863年9月30日)の政変：長州藩の急進的尊皇派、京都から追放される。

Coup D'etat of 30 September 1863: radical proimperial *samurai* of the Chōshū domain driven from Kyōto.

1864

天狗党の乱：水戸藩尊皇派の反乱。

Mito Civil War: proimperial uprising devastates the Mito domain.

池田屋事件：新撰組、長州藩士を中心とする尊皇派を京都池田屋におそう。

Ikedaya Incident: clash at the Ikedaya, an inn located in the center of Kyōto, between proimperial *samurai*, many from the Chōshū domain, and the shogunal Shinsengumi police force.

井伊直弼 **Ii Naosuke**

アメリカ合衆国で南北戦争(1861年〜 **1861**
1865年)はじまる。
Civil War begins in the United States
(1861–65).
イタリア統一。
Unification of Italy.

西周 **Nishi Amane**

カンボジア、フランスの保護国となる。 **1863**
Cambodia is made a protectorate of
France.

国際労働者協会(通称第1インターナショ **1864**
ナル)、ロンドンで結成。
The International Workingmen's
Association (commonly known as
the First International) is founded in
London.

64

蛤御門の変(禁門の変)：長州藩の急進的尊皇派上洛する；朝廷、幕府に長州征伐を命じる。

Hamaguri Gomon Incident (also known as the **Kimmon Incident**): proimperial Chōshū domain extremists attempt to force their way into Kyōto; the imperial court orders the shogunate to mount a punitive expedition against Chōshū (the first of the **Chōshū Expeditions**).

4国艦隊下関砲撃事件：欧米艦隊、下関海峡通過の外国船を砲撃した長州藩を攻撃。

Shimonoseki Bombardment: naval expedition by the Western powers against the Chōshū domain in retaliation for attacks on its ships passing through the Shimonoseki Strait.

1865 イギリス全権大使H＝S＝パークス、来日；後に日本研究家として有名になるE＝M＝サトーとW＝G＝アストンを通訳とする。

British minister plenipotentiary Sir Harry Smith Parkes arrives in Japan; Ernest Mason Satow and William George Aston, who later earn renown as Japanologists, serve him as interpreters.

1866 徳川幕府に対抗し**薩長同盟**成立。

Satsuma-Chōshū Alliance formed against the Tokugawa shogunate.

幕府、改税約書をイギリス・フランス・オランダ・アメリカと調印。

Kaizei Yakusho (**Tariff Convention**) signed with Great Britain, France, the Netherlands, and the United States.

幕府軍2度目の**長州征伐**；幕府軍は敗退し幕府の威信は著しく失墜する。

Shogunal army engages forces of the Chōshū domain in the second of the **Chōshū Expeditions**; the shogunate's failure to bring the campaign to a successful conclusion severely damages its prestige.

1867 大政奉還：最後の将軍徳川慶喜、朝廷に政権を返上。

Taisei Hōkan (**Return of Political Rule to the Emperor**): formal return of political authority to the emperor by the last shōgun, Tokugawa Yoshinobu.

明治時代 **Meiji period** (1868–1912)

明治維新によって天皇制国家に転換し明治時代がはじまり、近代産業社会への改革がはじまった。維新の指導者は、封建的藩体制を廃止して近代的国家に統合し、中央集権的官僚制度、新しい土地税制、徴兵による近代的軍隊を実施した。封建的な身分制度は廃止になり普通教育も制度化されて、統一国家としての体制が徐々に整った。1889年には大日本帝国憲法が発布されて、アジアで最初の議会政治が始まった。明治時代も後半になると日本は、日清・日露の戦争で勝利をおさめ、されに1910年には韓国を併合して、世界の帝国主義勢力の一つにのし上った。

徳川慶喜 **Tokugawa Yoshinobu**

A＝ノーベル、イギリスでダイナマイト
の特許をとる。 **1867**
Alfred Nobel patents dynamite in
Great Britain.

カール＝マルクス、ベルリンで「資本論」
の第1巻を出版。
Karl Marx publishes the first volume
of *Das Kapital* in Berlin.

The Meiji Restoration of direct imperial rule commenced the Meiji
period and began Japan's transformation into a modern industrial
society. Restoration leaders welded former feudal domains into a
modern nation-state, established a centralized bureaucracy, enacted
a new land tax system, and created a modern conscript army.
Abolition of feudal classes and the establishment of universal
education helped create a unified national polity. The 1889
Constitution of the Empire of Japan established the first
parliamentary government in Asia. During the latter part of the
period Japan emerged as a major imperialist power through
victories in the Sino-Japanese War of 1894–1895 and the Russo-
Japanese War and the annexation of Korea in 1910.

1868

王政復古(慶応3年12月9日)：明治維新はじまる。

Restoration of Imperial Rule (3 January 1868); Meiji Restoration is initiated.

戊辰戦争(1868年～1869年)：旧幕府諸軍、一連の戦いに敗れる。

Boshin Civil War (1868–69): shogunate loyalist forces are defeated in a series of battles.

明治天皇、五箇条を誓約；「五榜の掲示」公布。

Charter Oath (Imperial Oath of Five Articles) promulgated by **Emperor Meiji**; Gobō no Keiji (**Five Public Notices**) issued.

神仏分離：神社の仏僧(別当・社僧)に還俗するよう命令。

Separation of Shintō and Buddhism: buddhist priests serving at Shintō shrines are ordered to abandon their vows and return to the laity.

政体書公布。

Seitaisho (**Constitution of 1868** or Organic Act) issued.

太政官明治新政府の中心機関となる。

Dajōkan (**Grand Council of State**) becomes the central organ of the new imperial government.

明治政府、最初の紙幣太政官札を発行。

First national paper currency, Dajōkan *satsu*, issued.

江戸を東京と改める：翌年正式に首都となる。

The city of Edo is renamed Tōkyō ("eastern capital"); it becomes the official seat of government the following year.

天皇、元号を明治とする。

The emperor adopts the **era name** (*gengō*) Meiji ("**Enlightened Rule**").

天皇、東京行幸を行う；翌年、正式に皇居を京都から新首都に移す。

The emperor makes a preliminary visit to Tōkyō; he formally moves his residence from Kyōto to the new capital the following year.

1869

版籍奉還：藩の領有権を明治天皇に返還。

Hanseki hōkan: **formal return of domainal registers** to Emperor Meiji.

東京招魂社(現在の靖国神社)創建。戊辰戦争の戦死者を合祀。

Shōkonsha (**Shrine for Inviting the Spirits**; now Yasukuni Shrine or **Shrine for Establishing Peace in the Empire**) is established in Tōkyō, venerating all those who had died in the **Boshin Civil War**.

蝦夷地、北海道と改称。開拓使設置。

Ezochi is renamed Hokkaidō; the Kaitakushi (**Hokkaidō Colonization Office**) is opened.

1870

東京・横浜間に電信開通。

Telegraph line links Tōkyō and Yokohama.

大教宣布の詔を発し、神道を国家統一の基盤とすることを示す。

Imperial rescript (the Daikyō Sempu) declares Shintō beliefs to be the basis for national unity.

平民、苗字の使用を許される。

Commoners (*heimin*) are permitted to assume surnames.

1871

日本初の邦字日刊紙「横浜毎日新聞」創刊。

First Japanese-language daily newspaper, *Yokohama mainichi shimbun*, begins publication.

スペイン、共和制(1873年～1874年)になるが短命に終る。
Short-lived first Spanish republic (1873–74) established.

1873

最初の太陽暦
First Gregorian Calendar in Japan

御雇外国人
Foreign Employees of the Meiji Period

ベル、電話を発明。
The first successful telephone transmission is achieved by Alexander Graham Bell.

1876

廃刀令公布：帯刀を禁止。

Haitōrei: edict issued prohibiting the wearing of swords.

E=ベルツ、東京医学校(東京大学医学部の前身)生理学の教師として来日；1902年宮内省侍医となる。

Erwin von Bälz arrives in Japan to teach physiology at Tōkyō University Medical School; in 1902 he becomes **physician-in-waiting to the imperial household**.

W=S=クラーク来日、札幌農学校(現在、北海道大学の一部)の教頭となる。

William Smith Clark arrives in Japan to serve as the vice president of **Sapporo Agricultural College** (now part of Hokkaidō University).

士族、神風連の乱、秋月の乱、萩の乱を起こす。

Jimpūren Rebellion, Akizuki Rebellion of 1876, Hagi Rebellion mounted by discontented former *samurai (shizoku)*.

茨城県と三重県で農民、地租改正反対の一揆をおこす；翌年地租引下げ実施。

Uprisings in Ibaraki and Mie prefectures by peasants who demand a land tax reduction; lower rates implemented in 1877.

1877　西南戦争；西郷隆盛自害。

Satsuma Rebellion; Saigō Takamori commits suicide.

英国聖公会宣教師J=バチェラー来日；「アイヌ英和対訳辞典」(1889年)を出版。

Anglican missionary John Batchelor arrives in Japan; in 1889 he publishes *An Ainu English Japanese Dictionary*.

1878　内務卿大久保利通、石川県士族に暗殺される。

Home Minister Ōkubo Toshimichi assassinated by disaffected former *samurai (shizoku)* of Ishikawa Prefecture.

E=F=フェノロサ来日、東京大学で哲学と理財学を教える；西洋に日本の伝統美術を紹介し、国内における日本美術の再評価に貢献。

Ernest Francisco Fenollosa arrives in Japan to teach philosophy and political economy at Tōkyō University; he will eventually bring an appreciation of traditional Japanese art to the West and contribute to the reassessment of Japanese art within Japan.

竹橋騒動、約260名の近衛兵が反乱。

Takehashi Insurrection by some 260 government solders.

1879　琉球、沖縄県として日本に組み入れられる。

Part of the Ryūkyū Islands incorporated into Japan as Okinawa Prefecture.

1880　国会期成同盟結成。

Formation of the **League for Establishing a National Assembly**.

集会条例公布；自由民権運動を弾圧。

Shūkai Jōrei (**Public Assembly Ordinance**) issued to control the **Freedom and People's Rights Movement**.

1881　開拓使官有物払下げ事件。

Hokkaidō Colonization Office Scandal of 1881.

明治14年の政変：大隈重信失脚。

Political Crisis of 1881: expulsion of Ōkuma Shigenobu from the government.

10年後の憲法公布と国会開設を約束した勅諭発布。

Imperial rescript promises the promulgation of a constitution and the convening of a national assembly within a decade.

フェノロサ, E=F
Ernest Francisco Fenollosa

大英帝国ヴィクトリア女王、インド皇帝 **1877**
を兼ねる。
Queen Victoria crowned empress of
India.

首里城 (1933年)
Shuri Castle

日本最初の政党、**自由党**結成。

Jiyūtō (**Liberal Party**), Japan's first national political party, is formed.

松方正義、大蔵卿に就任。松方財政に着手。

Matsukata Masayoshi becomes minister of finance and begins to implement the **Matsukata fiscal policy**.

1882

立憲改進党結成。

Rikken Kaishintō (**Constitutional Reform Party**) founded.

日本銀行設立。

Bank of Japan established.

壬午事変：日本式軍制改革に反発し、朝鮮の旧式軍隊の兵士が反乱。この結果済物浦条約を調印し、朝鮮は日本に賠償金の支払いとソウルの公使館保護のための駐兵権を認める。

Imō Mutiny: revolt of traditionalist Korean troops in reaction to the Japanese-inspired modernization of the Korean army. In the **Treaty of Chemulp'o**, signed later that year, Korea agrees to pay an indemnity and the costs of stationing a Japanese legation guard in Seoul.

西欧の翻訳詩を含む最初の近代詩集「**新体詩抄**」出版。

Publication of the *Shintaishi shō* (**Collection of New-Style Poetry**), the first poetry anthology to include translations of Western verse.

1883

J=コンドル設計、煉瓦造り2階建て洋館・**鹿鳴館**が完成；外国貴賓や上流社会の西洋式社交場となる。

Completion of the Rokumeikan (**Deer Cry Pavilion**), a two-story brick building designed by Josiah Conder; it is the site for Western-style social events attended by prominent Japanese and foreigners.

1884

華族令公布：508名が華族になる。

Peerage Act issued: 508 titles of nobility conferred.

加波山事件：自由党の過激派、茨城県加波山にて警官隊と衝突。

Kabasan Incident: radical members of the Jiyūtō (**Liberal Party**) clash with police and government troops in the Mt. Kaba region, Ibaraki Prefecture.

秩父事件：埼玉県秩父地方の農民、**自由民権運動**の指導者に率いられ反政府の反乱を起こす。

Chichibu Incident: peasants in the Chichibu region of Saitama Prefecture, led by members of the **Freedom and People's Rights Movement**, rise against the government.

日本軍の支援の下、朝鮮にて**甲申事変**起こる。

Kapsin Political Coup mounted in Korea with the support of Japanese.

1885

日本で最初の**ハワイ移民**、出発。

First group of Japanese **emigrants to Hawaii** departs.

天津条約：朝鮮における利益をめぐって、日清間で結ばれる。

Tianjin Convention: agreement reached between China and Japan concerning their interests in Korea.

大阪事件：朝鮮におけるクーデター計画の首謀者、逮捕、処罰される。

Ōsaka Incident: leaders of a plot to mount a coup d'état in Korea arrested and tried.

松方正義 **Matsukata Masayoshi**

日本銀行本店
Meiji-Period Building of the Bank of Japan

フランスで無料の初等義務教育が制度化。

Tuition-free compulsory elementary education instituted in France.

1882

清仏戦争(1883年〜1885年)はじまる；中国、フランスのヴェトナム保護権を認める(1885年)。

Sino-French War (1883–85) begins; in 1885 China recognizes Vietnam as a protectorate of France.

1883

鹿鳴館
Rokumeikan (Deer Cry Pavilion)

内閣制度制定：内閣、太政官に代わり国務遂行の中心機関となる。

Cabinet system adopted; the new cabinet supersedes the Dajōkan (**Grand Council of State**) as the central organ of the Japanese state.

1886

ノルマントン号事件：イギリス貨物船ノルマントン号の日本人乗客23人全員が死亡；イギリス人乗組員は救命ボートで脱出。

Normanton **Incident**: all 23 Japanese passengers on the British freighter *Normanton* drown; the British crew escape in lifeboats.

1887

二葉亭四迷、日本初の近代小説「浮雲」の連載を始める。

Futabatei Shimei begins publication of *Ukigumo* (**Drifting Clouds**), a work regarded as Japan's first modern novel.

大同団結運動、議会開設に備え各政党の改革団結を求める。

Daidō Danketsu Movement (**"Larger Common Purpose" Movement**) seeks reorganization of political parties in preparation for the establishment of a parliamentary system.

三大事件建白運動、西欧諸国との不平等条約改正を提案。

Sandai Jiken Kempaku Movement (**Movement to Memorialize Three Important Items**) proposes revision of the **Unequal Treaties** with the Western powers.

保安条例制定、民権運動の弾圧を目的とする。

Peace Preservation Law of 1887 issued to suppress political agitation.

1888

枢密院設置。

Privy Council established.

磐梯山噴火；444人死亡。

The volcano Bandaisan erupts; 444 people die.

1889

大日本帝国憲法(明治憲法)発布。

Constitution of the Empire of Japan (Meiji Constitution) promulgated.

皇室典範制定。

Imperial Household Law enacted.

1890

森鴎外、短編「舞姫」を出版；近代日本文学における巨匠の登場。

Mori Ōgai publishes the short story "Maihime" (**The Dancing Girl**); this marks the debut of a major voice in modern Japanese literature.

L＝ハーン、東京に到着；「知られざる日本の面影」(1894年)を出版し、日本に関する著述家として名声を築く。

Lafcadio Hearn arrives in Tōkyō; *Glimpses of an Unfamiliar Japan* (1894; tr *Shirarezaru Nihon no omokage*) will establish his reputation as a writer on Japan.

初めての総選挙。

First **general election**.

教育勅語、全国の学校に配布。

Imperial Rescript on Education distributed to all schools.

第1回帝国議会召集。

First session of the **Imperial Diet** convened.

北里柴三郎、ドイツのE＝ベーリングと共同研究でジフテリアと破傷風の血清療法を発見。

Kitasato Shibasaburō cooperates with Emil Behring in Germany in developing serum therapies for the treatment of diphtheria and tetanus.

二葉亭四迷 **Futabatei Shimei**

イギリス、ビルマを併合。
Britain annexes Burma.

1886

大日本帝国憲法発布式典
Promulgation Ceremony of the Constitution of the Empire of Japan

パリで開かれた第2インターナショナル、メーデーを国際労働者の日と宣言。
The Second Socialist International, meeting in Paris, declares May Day an international labor day.

1889

北里柴三郎 **Kitasato Shibasaburō**

1891   大津事件：観光のため来日中のロシア皇太子 N＝アレクサンドロヴィッチ
       大津で襲撃される。

Ōtsu Incident; assassination attempt on Russian Crown Prince
Nicholas Alexandrovitch, who is on a pleasure tour of Japan.

岐阜県と愛知県で大地震（濃尾大地震）；7273人死亡。

Earthquake in Gifu and Aichi prefectures (Nōbi Earthquake); 7,273
people die.

田中正造、足尾鉱毒事件に関する質問書を議会に提出。

Tanaka Shōzō submits query to the Diet concerning the **Ashio
Copper Mine Incident**.

1892   出口ナオ、大本教を開く。

Deguchi Nao founds the religious sect Ōmoto.

1893   東学党の乱(甲午農民戦争)；朝鮮で農民反乱。(1894年清と日本が介入し、
       日清戦争はじまる。)

Tonghak Rebellion, a peasant uprising, breaks out in Korea. (China
and Japan intervene in 1894, commencing the **Sino-Japanese War of
1894–1895**).

画家黒田清輝、留学先のパリから帰国し日本に印象主義を紹介。

Artist Kuroda Seiki returns from study in Paris and introduces
impressionism to Japan.

1894   日英通商航海条約調印。1866年の改税約書(関税協定)調印国との最初の条
       約改正。治外法権を撤廃し、関税自主権を部分的に回復。

Anglo-Japanese Commercial Treaty of 1894 signed; the first treaty
revision with a signatory of the Kaizei Yakusho (**Tariff Convention**)
of 1866, it abolishes extraterritoriality and restores partial tariff
autonomy to Japan.

日清戦争(1894年～1895年)はじまる。

Sino-Japanese War of 1894–1895 begins.

1895   下関条約調印；日清講和する。

Treaty of Shimonoseki ends hostilities between China and Japan.

3国干渉：ロシア・フランス・ドイツ日本に満州南部の遼東半島の返還を
勧告。

Tripartite Intervention: Japan forced by Russia, France, and Germany
to relinquish the **Liaodong Peninsula** in southern Manchuria.

日清戦争の講和条件によって台湾が日本の植民地となる。

Taiwan becomes a Japanese colony as part of China's terms of
surrender at the end of the **Sino-Japanese War of 1894–1895**.

日本軍、朝鮮の王妃閔紀を暗殺。

Assassination of **Queen Min** of Korea by Japanese troops.

1897   日本人が経営、編集した初の英字新聞「ジャパンタイムズ」の刊行始まる。

Japan Times, the first English-language newspaper owned and edited
by Japanese, commences publication.

初の近代的労働者団体、職工義友会設立。

Shokkō Giyūkai (**Workers' Fraternal Society**), Japan's first modern
labor organization, is founded.

1898   憲政党結成。

Kenseitō (**Constitutional Party**) formed.

田中正造 **Tanaka Shōzō**

ロシア皇帝アレクサンドル3世、シベリア横断鉄道の建設開始を発令。
Tsar Alexander III issues rescript initiating construction of the Trans-Siberian Railway.

1891

フランス、ラオスを併合。
France annexes Laos.

1893

黒田清輝「湖畔」
Kuroda Seiki's By the Lake

最初のオリンピック、アテネで開催。
First modern Olympic Games held at Athens.

1896

ロシア、中国(清)から大連と旅順を租借。
China leases Dalian and Port Arthur to Russia.
米西戦争；スペイン、フィリピン、グアム、プエルトリコをアメリカ合衆国に譲る。
Spanish-American War; Spain cedes the Philippines, Guam, and Puerto Rico to the United States.
アメリカ合衆国、ハワイを併合。
United States annexes Hawaii.

1898

社会主義研究会結成。
Shakai Shugi Kenkyūkai (**Society for the Study of Socialism**) formed.

1899

東京の歌舞伎座で初の国産映画(風景や芸者の舞踊)上映。
First Japanese-made motion picture (featuring scenery and *geisha* dances) shown at the Kabukiza theater in Tōkyō.

新渡戸稲造「武士道」をフィラデルフィアで出版。
Nitobe Inazō publishes **Bushido: The Soul of Japan** (tr *Bushidō*) in Philadelphia.

1900

治安警察法制定。
Public Order and Police Law of 1900 enacted.

詩誌「明星」、与謝野鉄幹主宰で刊行開始。
Poetry journal *Myōjō* (**Bright Star**) begins publication under the editorship of Yosano Tekkan.

軍部大臣現役武官制確立。陸・海軍大臣は現役の武官に限られる。
System of the *gumbu daijin gen'eki bukan sei* (**active duty officers as service ministers**) established under which only military men on active duty can serve as army or navy ministers.

中国(清)で義和団の乱；ロシア、満州を占領。日本のアジア大陸進出の野望くじかれる。
Boxer Rebellion in China; Russia occupies Manchuria, threatening Japanese colonial ambitions on the Asian continent.

伊藤博文、立憲政友会結成。
Rikken Seiyūkai (**Friends of Constitutional Government Party**) formed by Itō Hirobumi.

1901

超国家主義者、黒竜会を設立。日本のアジア大陸侵略に協力。
Ultranationalist **Amur River Society** founded to promote Japanese expansion in Asia.

社会民主党結成。
Shakai Minshutō (**Socialist Democratic Party**) formed.

与謝野晶子、情熱的な短歌集「乱れ髪」出版。
Yosano Akiko publishes *Midaregami* (tr **Tangled Hair**), a collection of passionate *tanka* verse.

八幡製鉄所操業開始。
Yawata Iron and Steel Works begins operation.

1902

日英同盟調印。
Anglo-Japanese Alliance signed.

教科書疑獄：文部省官吏など、出版社からの収賄で告発される。
Textbook Scandal of 1902–1903: government officials accused of accepting bribes from publishers.

1903

社会主義者団体、平民社結成。
Heiminsha (**Society of Commoners**), a socialist organization, founded.

1904

日露戦争(1904年～1905年)はじまる。
Russo-Japanese War (1904–05) begins.

幸徳秋水と堺利彦、社会主義を掲げる「平民新聞」に、K＝マルクスとF＝エンゲルス起草の「共産党宣言」の邦訳掲載。
Kōtoku Shūsui and Sakai Toshihiko publish the first Japanese translation of Karl Marx and Friedrich Engels's *Communist*

新渡戸稲造 **Nitobe Inazō**

与謝野晶子 **Yosano Akiko**

アメリカ国務長官ジョン＝ヘイ、中国 1899
(清)の「門戸開放」覚書をイギリス、ドイ
ツ、フランス、ロシア、イタリア、日本
に通告。
US secretary of state John Hay sends
his Open Door notes concerning
China to Great Britain, Germany,
France, Russia, Italy, and Japan.

ライト兄弟(ウィルバー、オーヴィル)は 1903
じめて動力飛行機による飛行に成功。
Wilbur and Orville Wright achieve
the first sustained flight in a power-
driven airplane.

Manifesto (tr *Kyōsantō sengen*) in their socialist newspaper *Heimin shimbun*.

G＝B＝サンソム来日；「日本文化小史」(1931年)と「日本史」(全3巻；1958年～1963年)を出版。

George Bailey Sansom arrives in Japan; he later publishes *Japan: A Short Cultural History* (1931) and the three-volume *History of Japan* (1958-63).

1905　夏目漱石、猫が語り手の風刺小説「我輩は猫である」の連載を雑誌「ホトトギス」上に始める。

Natsume Sōseki begins serialization in the magazine *Hototogisu* of *Wagahai wa neko de aru* (tr *I Am a Cat*), a satirical novel whose narrator is a cat.

日露戦争終了；ポーツマス条約調印。

Treaty of Portsmouth ends the **Russo-Japanese War**.

日比谷焼打事件：ポーツマス条約の条件に抗議して群衆が焼き打ち。

Hibiya Incendiary Incident: demonstrators protest the terms of the Treaty of Portsmouth.

第2次日韓協約：韓国を保護国化する。

Korean-Japanese Convention of 1905: Korea becomes a Japanese protectorate.

1906　韓国統監府設置。

Office of the **Resident General in Korea** established.

日本社会党結成；1907年結社禁止となる。

Japan Socialist Party formed; it is banned by the government in 1907.

島崎藤村、被差別部落出身の青年の苦悩を描いた自然主義小説「破戒」を出版。

Shimazaki Tōson publishes the naturalist novel *Hakai* (tr *The Broken Commandment*), which deals with the plight of a young man who is a member of an oppressed class.

岡倉覚三、ニューヨークで「茶の本」を出版。

Okakura Kakuzō publishes *The Book of Tea* (tr *Cha no hon*) in New York City.

日本人学童隔離：日本政府、サンフランシスコの学校で起きた隔離命令に抗議。

Segregation of Japanese schoolchildren in the United States: Japanese government protests the segregation of Japanese children in San Francisco schools.

南満州鉄道発足。

South Manchuria Railway incorporated.

1907　韓国統監伊藤博文、朝鮮皇帝高宗の退位と第3次日韓協約の調印を強制する。朝鮮の内政を事実上支配。

Itō Hirobumi, the **Japanese resident general in Korea**, forces Korean **King Kojong's** abdication and the signing of the **Korean-Japanese Convention of 1907**, giving Japan effective control of Korea's internal affairs.

1908　第1回ブラジル移民、神戸から出発。

First group of Japanese **emigrants to Brazil** departs from Kōbe.

高平・ルート協定：アメリカ、満州における日本の特別な地位を認める。

Takahira-Root Agreement: Japanese gains US recognition of its

夏目漱石 **Natsume Sōseki**

A＝アインシュタイン、特殊相対性理論
を発表。
Albert Einstein announces his special
theory of relativity.

1905

ポーツマス条約
Treaty of Portsmouth

岡倉覚三 **Okakura Kakuzō**

special status in Manchuria.

1909

イギリス人陶芸家 B=リーチ来日：著書「陶工の本」(1940年)で東アジアの上薬と窯の技術を西欧に紹介。

English potter Bernard Leach arrives in Japan; his *Potter's Book* (1940; tr *Tōkō no hon*) introduces East Asian glaze and kiln technology to the West.

東京市、2000本以上の桜の若木を親善のためワシントンへ寄贈。

Government of the city of Tōkyō gives more than 2,000 flowering cherry saplings as a goodwill present to Washington, DC.

伊藤博文、満州のハルビン駅頭で朝鮮民族主義者・安重根に暗殺される

Itō Hirobumi assassinated on his arrival at Harbin in Manchuria by Korean nationalist **An Chung-gǔn**.

1910

立憲国民党結成。

Rikken Kokumintō (**Constitutional Nationalist Party**) formed.

大逆事件：幸徳秋水、明治天皇暗殺計画に連座；翌年処刑される。

High Treason Incident of 1910: Kōtoku Shūsui implicated in a plot to assassinate Emperor Meiji; he is executed the following year.

民俗学者柳田国男、岩手県遠野地方の村の生活と伝承を研究した「遠野物語」を出版。

Folklorist Yanagita Kunio publishes *Tōno monogatari* (tr *The Legends of Tono*), a study of village life and lore in Tōno, Iwate Prefecture.

日韓併合：韓国、日本の植民地とされる；朝鮮総督府を置く。

Annexation of Korea: Korea is made a colony of Japan; **Government-General of Korea** established.

白瀬矗率いる遠征隊、南極大陸探検のため日本を出発。

Expedition headed by Shirase Nobu departs Japan to explore Antarctica.

石川啄木、最初の短歌集「一握の砂」を出版。

Ishikawa Takuboku publishes his first collection of *tanka* verse, *Ichiaku no suna* (tr *A Handful of Sand*).

1911

南北朝正閏論：南北朝(1337年～1392年)の正統性について政府で歴史論議起こる。

Nambokuchō *seijun ron*: government historical debate over the legitimacy of the imperial **Northern and Southern Courts** (1337–92).

哲学者西田幾多郎、「善の研究」を出版。

Philosopher Nishida Kitarō publishes *Zen no Kenkyū* (tr *A Study of Good*).

ヨーロッパ列強と関税自主権回復の条約に調印。

Treaties signed with the Western powers that restore tariff autonomy to Japan.

工場法制定；労働者を保護。

Factory Law of 1911 enacted to protect laborers.

平塚らいてう、フェミニスト団体「青鞜社」設立。

Feminist organization Seitōsha (**Bluestocking Society**) founded by Hiratsuka Raichō.

柳田国男 **Yanagita Kunio**

ノルウェーの探検家R＝アムンゼン、人 **1911**
類史上初めて南極点に到達。
Norwegian explorer Roald
Amundsen becomes first person to
reach the South Pole.

「青鞜」 **Seitō**

大正時代 Taishō period (1912–1926)

大正時代は本格的な政党内閣の出現、民衆の政治参加の拡大、労働運動や左翼運動の発展、第1次世界大戦の刺激による好景気等によって特徴づけられる。この時代の民主主義的傾向は大正デモクラシーとよばれ、新しく出現した都市の中流知識人層やラジオ、大新聞、雑誌、文庫本などの新しいマスメディアに支えられた。しかし経済の後退、治安維持法の制定、特別高等警察(特高)の強化拡大と共に日本ではじめて経験された民主主義も徐々に衰退していった。

1912 日本、ストックホルムで開催された第5回夏季オリンピックに選手2人を送る。

Japan sends two athletes to the 5th **Summer Olympic Games** at Stockholm.

明治天皇逝去。大正天皇即位。

Death of Emperor Meiji; accession of Emperor Taishō.

友愛会結成、労働者の組織化始まる。

Yūaikai (**Friendship Association**) formed; begins the organization of Japanese labor.

第1次憲政擁護運動、始まる。

First **Movement to Protect Constitutional Government** founded.

1913 大正政変：第3次桂太郎内閣、憲政擁護運動で倒される。

Taishō Political Crisis: third Katsura Tarō cabinet toppled by the Movement to Protect Constitutional Government.

1914 シーメンス事件：海軍高官が汚職で告発される：第1次山本権兵衛内閣総辞職。

Siemens Incident: naval authorities charged with bribery; resignation of the first Yamamoto Gonnohyōe cabinet.

日本、イギリスなど協商国側に立って第1次世界大戦に参戦。

Japan enters **World War I** on the side of Great Britain and its allies.

1915 日本、中国に対華21ヵ条要求提出、領土その他の利権を要求する。

Japan presents China with its **Twenty-One Demands** for territorial and other concessions.

1916 アジア初のノーベル文学賞受賞者 R＝タゴール、初来日。

Rabindranath Tagore, the first Asian to receive the **Nobel Prize for literature**, makes his first visit to Japan.

S＝エリセーエフ、サンクト＝ペテルベルグ大学の日本語講師に任命される；後にソルボンヌ大高等研究院およびハーバード大学教授となる。

Serge Elisséeff is appointed lecturer in Japanese as the University of St. Petersburg; he later becomes a professor at the Ecole des Hautes Etudes of the Sorbonne and at Harvard University.

The Taishō period was marked by the advent of true party government, increased popular involvement in politics, the growth of organized labor and left-wing movements, and a domestic economic boom fueled by World War I. The democratic tendencies of the period, often referred to as Taishō Democracy, were supported by the emergence of an educated urban middle class and the rise of new forms of mass media such as radio, large-circulation newspapers, magazines, and paperback books. Eventually, however, an economic downturn and authoritarian measures such as the enactment of the Peace Preservation Law of 1925 and the expansion of the Special Higher Police began to erode the gains made by Japan's first experiment with democracy.

大正天皇 **Emperor Taishō**

中華民国設立、孫逸仙(孫文)大統領に就任；皇帝溥儀退位。
Republic of China established with Sun Yat-sen (Son Issen) as president; Emperor Puyi abdicates.

1912

N＝ボーア、原子構造を解明する。
Niels Bohr clarifies the structure of the atom.

1913

オーストリア皇太子フランツ＝フェルディナンド、サラエボで暗殺される；第1次世界大戦はじまる。
Archduke Francis Ferdinand assassinated at Sarajevo; World War I begins.

パナマ運河開通。
Panama Canal completed.

1914

1917 石井・ランシング協定：アメリカと日本、中国の門戸解放政策を支持することで同意；アメリカは中国における日本の特殊権益を認める。(協定は1923年廃止)

Lansing-Ishii Agreement: the United States and Japan agree to uphold the **Open Door Policy** in China; Japan gains recognition of its "special interest in China" (the agreement is annulled in 1923).

1918 シベリア出兵(1918年〜1922年)開始。

Commencement of the **Siberian Intervention** (1918–22).

インフレ加速し、米騒動おきる。寺内正毅内閣崩壊。

Rice riots of 1918, provoked by spiraling inflation, lead to the collapse of the Terauchi Masatake cabinet.

1919 朝鮮で3・1独立運動(1919年〜1920年)、起こる；日本軍、徹底的に鎮圧。

Samil Independence Movement (1919–20) begins in Korea; it is viciously suppressed by the Japanese.

日本、第1次世界大戦の戦勝国としてベルサイユ条約に調印する。

As a victor nation in World War I, Japan is a signatory to the **Treaty of Versailles**.

有島武郎、自我に目覚めた女性の自己崩壊を描いた感傷的小説「或る女」を出版。

Arishima Takeo publishes the melodramatic novel *Aru onna* (tr *A Certain Woman*), which depicts the self-destruction of a strong-willed woman.

1920 国際連盟設立；日本常任理事国となる。

League of Nations established; Japan is granted permanent membership in the League Council.

森戸事件：東京帝国大学助教授森戸辰男、無政府主義者 P＝A＝クロポトキンの社会主義思想に関する論文を発表し、3ヵ月投獄される。

Morito Incident: Morito Tatsuo, an assistant professor at **Tōkyō Imperial University**, is imprisoned for three months for publishing an article on the social theory of the anarchist Peter Alekseevich Kropotkin.

尼港事件：黒竜江河口に近いニコラエフスク(尼港)在住の日本人、虐殺される。

Nikolaevsk Incident: Japanese residents of the town of Nikolaevsk near the mouth of the Amur River are massacred.

日本初のメーデー祝典のため、東京上野公園に労働運動家集まる。

Labor activists gather in Tōkyō's Ueno Park for the first celebration of **May Day** in Japan.

日本社会主義同盟結成；1921年、政府は解散を命令。

Nihon Shakai Shugi Dōmei (**Japan Socialist League**) founded; the government orders it to dissolve in 1921.

1921 志賀直哉、代表作「暗夜行路」の連載開始。

Shiga Naoya begins serialization of his masterwork, the novel *An'ya Kōro* (tr *A Dark Night's Passing*).

友愛会、総同盟となる。

Yūaikai (**Friendship Association**) becomes the Sōdōmei (**Japan Federation of Labor**).

ロシアで10月革命。
October Revolution in Russia.

シベリア出兵 Siberian Intervention

1917

モハンダス=ガンジー、インドで不服従
運動始める。
Mohandas K. Gandhi initiates a civil
disobedience campaign in India.
中国で5・4運動おきる；中国内のドイ
ツの権益と租借地を日本に譲渡のパリ平
和会議の決定に抗議する。
Participants in the May Fourth
Movement in China protest the
decision reached at the Paris Peace
Conference to award Germany's
rights and leases in China to Japan.

1919

米騒動 Rice Riots of 1918

アメリカ合衆国で女性に選挙権が認めら
れる。
Women granted suffrage in the
United States.

1920

志賀直哉 Shiga Naoya

総理大臣原敬、暗殺。

Prime Minister Hara Takashi assassinated.

ワシントン会議(1921年～1922年)はじまる；翌年**4ヵ国条約**、**9ヵ国条約**、ワシントン海軍軍縮条約成立。

Washington Conference (1921–22) begins; it will result in the signing of the **Four-Power Treaty**, the **Nine-Power Treaty**, and the **Washington Naval Treaty of 1922**.

皇太子裕仁(後の昭和天皇)、病弱な大正天皇の摂政となる。

Crown Prince Hirohito (later Emperor Shōwa) becomes regent to the ailing Emperor Taishō.

1922 水平社結成。

Suiheisha (**Society of Levelers**) founded.

日本共産党結成；度々政府に弾圧され、**第2次世界大戦**後まで非合法であった。

Japanese Communist Party established; frequently suppressed by the government, it is not legally constituted until after **World War II**.

F＝L＝ライト設計の**帝国ホテル**、完成。

Imperial Hotel, designed by Frank Lloyd Wright, is completed.

1923 関東大震災；マグニチュード7.9を記録。死者10万人以上。

Tōkyō Earthquake of 1923 (**Great Kantō Earthquake**); assigned a magnitude of 7.9, this earthquake resulted in more than 100,000 deaths.

虎ノ門事件：摂政裕仁の暗殺を計画。

Toranomon Incident: assassination attempt on Prince Regent Hirohito.

1924 第2次憲政擁護運動：護憲3派内閣成立。

Second **Movement to Protect Constitutional Government**; Goken Sampa Naikaku (**Cabinet of Three Groups Supporting the Constitution**) formed.

1925 日ソ基本条約に調印：日ソ間の外交関係、成立。

Soviet-Japanese Basic Convention signed: diplomatic relations between Japan and the Soviet Union established.

治安維持法公布。言論と集会の自由厳しく制限される。

Enactment of the **Peace Preservation Law of 1925**; freedoms of speech and assembly severely restricted.

普通選挙法成立(男子のみ)。

Universal Manhood Suffrage Law passed.

公共放送・NHKの前身、東京放送局がラジオ放送を開始。翌年NHK設立。

First regular radio broadcasting begun by the **Tōkyō Broadcasting Station**, a predecessor of Japan's public network, NHK, which was formed the following year.

太平洋問題調査会設立；1926年、国内組織の日本委員会を設立。

Institute of Pacific Relations established; its Japan Council is organized in 1926.

A＝D＝ウエーリー訳「源氏物語」(全6巻)第1巻を出版。

Arthur David Waley publishes the first volume of his six-volume translation of the *Tale of Genji*.

ムソリーニがイタリアにファシストと国
家主義者たちの政府を組織。
Benito Mussolini forms a cabinet of
Fascists and Nationalists in Italy.

1922

旧帝国ホテル
Original Imperial Hotel

関東大震災
Tōkyō Earthquake of 1923

昭和時代 Shōwa period (1926–1989)

昭和時代は日本史上最大の激動期の一つである。最初の20年間は右翼政治家と軍部からなる超国家主義者たちが国の指導権をにぎり、政治的弾圧を行いアジア大陸への軍事的拡張路線を敷いた。それは日中戦争(1937年～1945年)で頂点に達し、遂に第2次世界大戦へ突入した。敗戦により日本は連合国の占領下に置かれ、新しい日本国憲法の制定を含む徹底的な民主改革が行われた。戦後の数10年間で日本は国際社会に復帰し、驚異的な経済成長を成し遂げ、世界第2位の経済大国となった。

1926
労働農民党結成。
Rōdō Nōmintō (**Labor-Farmer Party**) formed.
社会民衆党結成。
Shakai Minshutō (**Socialist People's Party**) formed.
日本労農党結成。
Nihon Rōnōtō (**Japan Labor-Farmer Party**) formed.
大正天皇逝去；昭和天皇即位。
Death of Emperor Taishō; accession of Emperor Shōwa.

1927
金融恐慌。
Financial Crisis of 1927.
南京事件：南京の日・英・米の領事館、中国の国民革命軍に襲撃される。
Nanjing (Nanking) Incident: Japanese, British, and US consulates in Nanjing attacked by Chinese Nationalist soldiers.
第1次山東出兵：田中義一内閣、中国山東省に軍隊派遣。
First of the **Shandong (Shantung) Expeditions**: Tanaka Giichi cabinet dispatches troops to **Shandong Province** in China.

1928
3・15事件：1658人を共産主義者の嫌疑で検挙：このうち483人を起訴。
March 15th Incident: 1,658 suspected communists arrested; charges brought against 483.
満州の軍閥の首領張作霖、日本陸軍士官に暗殺される。
Manchurian warlord **Zhang Zuolin (Chang Tso-lin)** assassinated by Japanese army officers.
ケロッグ＝ブリアン条約(不戦条約)、日本を含む15ヵ国が調印：この条約の「其ノ各自の人民の名に於テ」という文言が天皇主権に触れるとして問題化した。
Kellogg-Briand Pact (in Japan called Fusen Jōyaku; "**Antiwar Treaty**") signed by Japan and 14 other countries; it provokes criticism in Japan for the use of the phrase "in the names of their respective peoples," which some Japanese take to be an assault on the sovereignty of the emperor.

The Shōwa period was one of the most turbulent in Japanese history. In its first decades an ultranationalist coalition of right-wing politicians and army officers seized control of the country, engaging in domestic political repression and setting Japan on a course of militarist expansionism in continental Asia that culminated in the Sino-Japanese War of 1937–45 and entry into World War II. Japan's defeat ushered in a period of Occupation by Allied military forces and sweeping democratic reforms that included a new Constitution of Japan. The postwar decades saw reentry into the international community and phenomenal economic growth that transformed Japan into the world's second largest economy by the end of the period.

昭和天皇 **Emperor Shōwa**

蒋介石、中国南京に国民政府樹立。
Chiang Kai-shek (Shō Kaiseki) sets up a Nationalist government in Nanjing.
チャールズ=リンドバーグ、大西洋を横断飛行する。
Charles Lindbergh flies across the Atlantic Ocean.

1927

1929

4・16事件：共産主義者の嫌疑で600人から700人が検挙され、339人が起訴される。

April 16th Incident: six hundred to 700 suspected communists arrested, charges brought against 339.

1930

昭和恐慌(1930年〜1935年)、始まる。

Shōwa Depression (1930–35) begins.

第1回の**ロンドン軍縮会議**；協定の海軍軍備制限に不満の海軍は、政府を激しく非難する(統帥権干犯問題)。

First of the **London Naval Conferences**; terms of the resulting naval arms limitation treaty provoke intense criticism of the government by the military.

日本最初の近代西洋美術館、**大原美術館**創立。

Ōhara Museum of Art, Japan's first museum of modern Western art, established.

浜口雄幸首相、東京駅にて右翼急進派に襲撃され重傷。

Prime Minister Hamaguchi Osachi mortally wounded at Tōkyō Station by a right-wing radical.

1931

3月事件：陸軍の右派過激派将校を中心とするグループ、クーデターを計画するが未遂に終わる。

March Incident: planned coup by rightist army officers and civilians aborted.

五所平之助、日本初の**トーキー映画**「マダムと女房」を監督し成功する。

Gosho Heinosuke directs Japan's first successful **sound film**, *Madamu to nyōbō* (**The Neighbor's Wife and Mine**).

柳条湖事件：関東軍による満州占領始まる(1931年〜1933年；満州事変)。

Liutiaohu (Liu-t'iao-hu) Incident: conquest of Manchuria by the Japanese **Guandong (Kwantung) Army** begins (1931–33; **Manchurian Incident**).

10月事件：軍のクーデター計画参加者検挙される。

October Incident: leaders of a planned military coup arrested.

1932

桜田門事件：昭和天皇暗殺計画。

Sakuradamon Incident: assassination attempt made on Emperor Shōwa.

上海事変：中国軍と日本軍、上海で武力衝突。

Shanghai Incident: Chinese and Japanese troops clash in Shanghai.

関東軍満州国を建国。清朝(1644年〜1912年)最後の皇帝溥儀が執政に就任(1934年皇帝に即位)。

Guandong (Kwantung) Army establishes the state of **Manchukuo**; the last **Qing dynasty** (1644–1912) emperor, **Puyi (P'u-i)**, is installed as chief executive of state (he is made emperor in 1934).

血盟団事件：過激な国家主義者団体血盟団、井上準之助、団琢磨を殺害。

League of Blood Incident: Inoue Junnosuke and Dan Takuma murdered by members of an **ultranationalist society**, the Ketsumeidan (**League of Blood**).

5・15事件：犬養毅首相海軍青年将校に暗殺される。

May 15th Incident: Prime Minister Inukai Tsuyoshi assassinated during an attempted coup by young naval officers.

アメリカで株式暴落、長期不況はじまる。 **1929**
US stock market crashes, prolonged
depression begins.

満州事変 **Manchurian Incident**

溥儀 **Puyi (P'u-i)**

犬養毅 **Inukai Tsuyoshi**

マルクス主義学者による、日本の資本主義発達の研究シリーズ「日本資本主義発達史講座」(1932年〜1933年；全7巻)出版始まる。

Nihon shihon shugi hattatsu shi kōza (1932–33; **Lectures on the History of the Development of Japanese Capitalism**; 7vols), a series of works of Marxist scholars dealing with the development of Japanese capitalism, begins publication.

愛国的女性組織、大日本国防婦人会結成。

Dai Nippon Kokubō Fujinkai (**National Defense Women's Association**), a patriotic women's organization, founded.

1933

日本、満州侵略を批判したリットン報告書に反対して、国際連盟を脱退。

Japan withdraws from the **League of Nations** to express its opposition to the report of the **Lytton Commission**, which criticizes Japan as an aggressor in Manchuria.

塘沽停戦協定：日中両軍、停戦協定を締結。

Tanggu (Tangku) Truce: armistice agreement between Chinese officials and officers of the Japanese **Guandong (Kwantung) Army**.

神兵隊事件：クーデター計画、指導者検挙される。

Shimpeitai Incident ("Divine Soldiers" Incident): leaders of a planned coup arrested.

小林多喜二、特高に拷問により殺される。

Kobayashi Takiji tortured to death by the Special Higher Police.

1934

帝人事件：政府高官、株不正事件に関わる。

Teijin Incident: government officials implicated in a stock scandal.

日本、ワシントン海軍軍縮条約を破棄。

Washington Naval Treaty of 1922 abrogated by Japan.

1935

天皇機関説：天皇の憲法上の地位に関する論議起こる。

Tennō kikan setsu (**Emperor-as-Organ-of-the-State Theory**): controversy arises over the constitutional status of the emperor.

梅津・何応欽協定、中国華北で結ばれる。

He-Umezu (Ho-Umezu) Agreement concluded in North China.

芥川賞と直木賞が制定される。

The prestigious literary awards **Akutagawa Prize** and **Naoki Prize** instituted.

1936

第2回のロンドン軍縮会議；日本、英米との軍備平等権を要求したが、認められず脱退を通告。

Second of the **London Naval Conferences**; Japan withdraws after rejection of its proposal that the Japanese fleet be granted full parity with the fleets of Britain and the United States.

2・26事件：1,400名の兵が参加したが失敗。

February 26th Incident: 1,400 troops participate in an unsuccessful coup d'état.

メーデー禁止される。

Observance of **May Day** prohibited in Japan.

1937

川端康成「雪国」・永井荷風「濹東綺譚」、単行本で出版される。

Publication in book form of the novels *Yukiguni* (tr *Snow Country*) by Kawabata Yasunari and *Bokutō kitan* (tr *A Strange Tale from East of the River*) by Nagai Kafū.

小林多喜二　**Kobayashi Takiji**

ヒットラー、ドイツ首相に就任。
Adolf Hitler becomes chancellor of
Germany.

1933

2・26事件　**February 26th Incident**

西安事件；張学良率いる満州軍、蒋介石
を監禁；共産党指導者が蒋介石を救出
し、民族主義者と共産主義者は日本の侵
略に対する協力で一致する。
Xi'an (Sian) Incident: troops of
Manchurian warlord Zhang Xueliang
detain Chiang Kai-shek; Communist
leaders effect his release, and
cooperation between Nationalists
and Communists against Japanese
aggression is agreed upon.

1936

盧溝橋事件：日中戦争(1937年～1945年)はじまる。

Marco Polo Bridge Incident: Sino-Japanese War of 1937–1945 commences.

南京虐殺事件(1937年～1938年)：日本軍南京占領、推定約14万人の一般住民・捕虜を虐殺。

Nanjing (Nanking) Massacre (1937–38): some 140,000 Chinese civilians and prisoners of war are estimated to have been murdered by Japanese forces following the taking of Nanjing.

人民戦線事件(1937年～1938年)：学者・文化人・反ファシズム運動家など400余名、検挙される。

Popular Front Incident (1937–38): some 400 liberals and leftists arrested.

1938 東亜新秩序：近衛文麿首相、「国民政府対手とせず声明」を発表、「東アジアにおける新しい秩序の確立」を表明。

Tōa Shinchitsujo (**"New Order in East Asia"**): Prime Minister Konoe Fumimaro declares a policy of nonrecognition of Nationalist China and calls for "the establishment of a **new order in East Asia**."

日本軍の南京占領について描く石川達三の短編「生きてゐる兵隊」発禁になる。

Ikite iru heitai (**Living Soldiers**), a novella by Ishikawa Tatsuzō dealing with the taking of Nanjing by Japanese forces, is banned.

国家総動員法公布。

Passage of the **National Mobilization Law**.

1939 ノモンハン事件：満州国とモンゴルの国境付近で日本軍、ソ連軍と激しく戦闘、日本軍の大敗に終わる。

Nomonhan Incident: heavy fighting between Japanese and Soviet troops along the Manchurian-Mongolian border ends in a rout of Japanese forces.

国民徴用令発布：軍需産業に労働力確保のため。

National Service Draft Ordinance issued to assure an adequate supply of labor in strategic industries.

1940 津田左右吉の批判的な日本古代史研究「神代史の研究」など発禁になる。

Tsuda Sōkichi's revisionist study of the prehistory of Japan, *Jindaishi no kenkyū*, is banned.

日独伊三国同盟調印。

Tripartite Pact signed by Japan, Germany, and Italy.

大政翼賛会発足。

Imperial Rule Assistance Association formed.

正倉院の宝物初公開。

Treasures of the Shōsōin are publicly exhibited for the first time.

1941 国民学校の義務教育制度発足：「皇国民の錬成」をねらいとする。

Compulsory school system of *kokumin gakkō* (**national people's schools**) established to train "**loyal subjects of the emperor**."

日ソ中立条約調印。

Soviet-Japanese Neutrality Pact signed.

駐米大使野村吉三郎とアメリカ国務長官ハル、行き詰まった日米関係打破をめざして話し合い開始。

Talks between Ambassador Nomura Kichisaburō and **Secretary of**

盧溝橋 **Marco Polo Bridge**

近衛文麿 **Konoe Fumimaro**

ドイツがポーランド侵入、ヨーロッパで 1939
第2次世界大戦(1939年〜1945年)はじま
る。
Germany invades Poland; World
War II (1939–1945) begins in Europe.

State Cordell Hull begin in an attempt to resolve the stalemate in US-Japan relations.

ゾルゲ事件：ドイツ人ジャーナリストR＝ゾルゲと尾崎秀実、ソ連の対日諜報活動に従事し、検挙・起訴される。

Sorge Incident: German journalist Richard Sorge and Japanese journalist Ozaki Hotsumi are taken into custody by the Tōkyō police and charged with spying for the Soviet Union.

太平洋戦争始まる：日本、真珠湾、マレー半島、フィリピンを攻撃：アメリカ合衆国、イギリス、オランダに宣戦布告。

Pacific War commences: Japanese attack **Pearl Harbor**, the Malay Peninsula, and the Philippines; war declared against the United States, Great Britain, and the Netherlands.

1942　日本軍、フィリピン・マライヤ・シンガポール・オランダ領東インド諸島を占領。

Japanese forces occupy the Philippines, Malaya, Singapore, the **Dutch East Indies**, and Burma.

連合艦隊、ミッドウェー海戦で敗れる。

Japanese **naval fleet** defeated in the **Battle of Midway**.

関門海峡に鉄道海底トンネル完成、下関と北九州をつなぐ。

Railway tunnel completed beneath the Kammon Strait connecting Shimonoseki and Kita Kyūshū.

1943　日本軍、ガダルカナル島から撤退。

Japanese forces withdraw from **Guadalcanal**.

中産階級の4人姉妹を描いた谷崎潤一郎の小説「細雪」の連載、軍の圧力で発禁となる。

Serialization of *Sasameyuki* (tr *The Makioka Sisters*), Tanizaki Jun'ichirō's novel about four upper-middle-class sisters, is suspended under pressure from the military.

海軍大将山本五十六死去。

Death of Admiral Yamamoto Isoroku.

アリューシャン列島のアッツ島で、日本軍玉砕。

Japanese forces on the island of **Attu** in the Aleutians annihilated.

弥生時代後期(100年～300年頃)の登呂遺跡、発見される。

Late-Yayoi-period (ca AD 100–ca AD 300) **Toro site** discovered.

1944　サイパン陥落。アメリカの大規模本土空襲始まる。

Saipan falls; large-scale US bombing raids on the Japanese main islands begin.

連合艦隊、レイテ沖海戦(比島沖海戦)で敗れる。

Japanese **naval fleet** defeated in the **Battle of Leyte Gulf** (also known in Japan as the **Battle off the Philippines**).

1945　硫黄島陥落。

Battle of Iōjima (Iwojima): Iōjima falls.

沖縄陥落。

Okinawa falls.

原子爆弾、広島・長崎に投下される。

Atomic bomb dropped on Hiroshima and Nagasaki.

日本ポツダム宣言受諾。

Japan accepts the terms of the **Potsdam Declaration**.

ゾルゲ, R **Richard Sorge**

山本五十六 **Yamamoto Isoroku**

ナチス党幹部、ワンゼー会議にて「ユダ **1942**
ヤ人」問題の「最終的解決」を計画する。
Nazi bureaucrats plan "final
solution" of the "Jewish question" at
the Wannsee Conference.

原子爆弾 **Atomic Bomb**

サンフランシスコで、50ヵ国の代表によ **1945**
り国連憲章が調印される：1956年、日
本加盟。
United Nations Charter signed at
San Francisco by delegates from 50
nations; Japan joins in 1956.

玉音放送；昭和天皇、国民に対して自らの声で終戦を宣言。

Imperial Broadcast: Emperor Shōwa announces the end of hostilities in a national radio broadcast.

連合国最高司令官(**SCAP**)ダグラス＝マッカーサー、日本占領(1945年～1952年)を指揮するため厚木飛行場に到着。

Douglas MacArthur, **supreme commander for the Allied powers (SCAP)**, arrives at **Atsugi Airfield** near Tōkyō to oversee the **Occupation** of Japan (1945–52).

降伏文書、米戦艦ミズーリ号上で調印。

Instrument of Surrender signed aboard the USS *Missouri*.

連合国最高司令官本部、日本人戦犯の逮捕を命じ、政治犯釈放・財閥解体等、日本の民主化に向けた覚書を交付。

SCAP headquarters orders the arrest of suspected Japanese **war criminals**, issues directives aimed at the democratization of Japan that include the release of **political prisoners** and the breakup of industrial and financial combines (**zaibatsu dissolution**).

日本社会党・日本共産党、再建。

Revival of the **Japan Socialist Party** and the **Japanese Communist Party**.

改正選挙法公布；婦人参政権実現。

Revised election law promulgated; women given the vote.

労働組合法公布。

Labor Union Law issued.

1946

昭和天皇、年頭の挨拶で神格否定し人間宣言。

Renunciation of divinity: Emperor Shōwa renounces his divinity in New Year's address to the Japanese people.

公職追放：戦前・戦中の指導者、公職から追放。

Occupation Purge of prewar and wartime Japanese leaders.

農地改革はじまる。

Implementation of the **Land Reforms of 1946** begins.

連合国最高司令官、インフレ抑制のための金融緊急措置令を公布；新円通貨切換。

Emergency anti-inflation measures issued by **SCAP**; "new yen" currency reform.

昭和天皇の国内巡幸を始まる。

Emperor Shōwa begins a series of goodwill tours of the country.

最初のアメリカ教育使節団到着。

First of the **United States education missions to Japan** arrives.

極東国際軍事裁判(東京裁判；1946年～1948年)開廷。

Commencement of the **International Military Tribunal for the Far East** (Tōkyō Trial; 1946–48).

食料メーデー：皇居前を30万人がデモ。

Shokuryō Mēdē (**Food May Day**): 300,000 people demonstrate in front of the Imperial Palace.

経団連(経済団体連合会)設立。

Formation of Keidanren (**Federation of Economic Organizations**).

ダグラス=マッカーサー
Douglas MacArthur

アメリカ大統領トルーマン、ソ連首相スターリン、イギリス首相チャーチル、ポツダム宣言で日本に無条件降伏を要求。

US president Harry Truman, Soviet premier Joseph Stalin, and British prime minister Winston Churchill call for the unconditional surrender of Japan in the Potsdam Declaration.

スカルノとモハマド=ハッタ、インドネシア共和国の独立を宣言。

Sukarno and Mohammad Hatta proclaim the independence of the Republic of Indonesia.

ホー=チ=ミン、ベトナムの独立を宣言。

Ho Chi Minh proclaims the independence of Vietnam.

昭和天皇の国内巡幸
Goodwill Tours of Emperor Shōwa

1946

マヌエル=ロハス、初代フィリピン共和国大統領に就任。

Republic of the Philippines inaugurated with Manuel Roxas as its first president.

ユネスコ設立される；1951年、日本加盟。

UNESCO established; Japan joins in 1951.

東京裁判 **Tōkyō Trial**

日本国憲法公布、翌年施行。

Constitution of Japan promulgated; it goes into effect in 1947.

相沢忠洋、**岩宿遺跡**を発見。日本ではじめて旧石器時代の遺跡を確認。

Aizawa Tadahiro discovers the **Iwajuku site**, the first recognized paleolithic site in Japan.

R=F=ベネディクト、日本人を社会学的に分析した「**菊と刀**」を出版。

Ruth Fulton Benedict publishes *The Chrysanthemum and the Sword* (tr *Kiku to katana*), a sociological study of the Japanese.

1947

連合国最高指令官、**2・1スト**を禁止。

SCAP bans the **General Strike of 1947**.

教育基本法・**労働基準法**・**独占禁止法**・**地方自治法**・**児童福祉法**制定。

Enactment of the **Fundamemtal Law of Education**, the **Labor Standards Law**, the **Antimonopoly Law**, the **Local Autonomy Law**, and the **Child Welfare Law**.

太宰治、小説「**斜陽**」を出版。

Dazai Osamu publishes the novel *Shayō* (tr *The Setting Sun*).

1948

日経連(日本経営者団体連盟)設立。

Nikkeiren (**Japan Federation of Employers' Associations**) founded.

昭電事件：政府高官、収賄罪で逮捕される。

Shōwa Denkō Scandal: government officials charged with the receipt of bribes.

優生保護法制定；妊娠中絶、優生手術などを規定。

Eugenic Protection Law enacted; it contains provisions governing abortion and sterilization.

経済安定9原則公布。

Nine Principles for Economic Stabilization issued.

1949

ドッジ=ライン：包括的インフレ対策導入；1ドル=360円の固定為替レート設定。

Dodge Line: comprehensive anti-inflation measures introduced; a **constant exchange rate** of ¥360 to US $1 established.

平事件・**下山事件**・**三鷹事件**・**松川事件**：一連の事件は破壊活動との関連を疑われ**日本共産党**世論の支持を失う；**占領政策の重点、民主化から経済成長**に変わる。

Taira Incident; **Shimoyama Incident**; **Mitaka Incident**; **Matsukawa Incident**: a succession of incidents that are either subversive or suspected of being subversive; public opinion turns against the **Japanese Communist Party**; emphasis of **Occupation** reforms shifts from democratization to **economic growth**.

シャウプ使節団、日本の税制に勧告；現在の**直接税**制度の基盤を築く。

Shoup mission gives recommendations on Japan's tax structure; foundation laid for the present system of **direct taxation**.

湯川秀樹**ノーベル物理学賞**受賞；日本人初のノーベル賞受賞。

Yukawa Hideki awarded the **Nobel Prize for physics**; he is the first Japanese to receive a Nobel Prize.

1950

自由党結成。

Jiyūtō (**Liberal Party**) formed.

公職選挙法制定。

Public Office Election Law enacted.

日本国憲法 Constitution of Japan

パキスタンとインド、独立。
Pakistan and India become sovereign nations.

1947

朝鮮半島に大韓民国、朝鮮民主主義人民共和国成立。
Republic of Korea established in the southern part of the Korean Peninsula and the Democratic People's Republic of Korea in the north.

1948

下山事件 Shimoyama Incident

北太西洋条約機構(NATO)設立。
North Atlantic Treaty Organization (NATO) founded.
中華人民共和国成立。
People's Republic of China established.

1949

湯川秀樹 Yukawa Hideki

朝鮮戦争(1950年〜1953年)はじまる。
Korean War begins (1950–1953).

1950

総評(日本労働組合総評議会)設立。

Sōhyō (**General Council of Trade Unions of Japan**) founded.

レッド＝パージ：1177人の共産党員の公務員を職場から追放。

Red Purge: 1,177 government employees who are **Japanese Communist Party** members removed from their positions.

警察予備隊創設。

National Police Reserve created.

1951

サンフランシスコ平和条約・日米安全保障条約調印。

San Francisco Peace Treaty and the first of the **United States-Japan security treaties** signed.

1952

日米行政協定調印。

United States-Japan Administrative Agreement signed.

サンフランシスコ平和条約発効；占領体制終わる。日本主権を回復。

San Francisco Peace Treaty goes into effect; Occupation ends and Japan regains its sovereignty.

メーデー事件：デモ参加者1232人、騒擾罪により検挙。

May Day Incident: 1,232 demonstrating workers arrested under the **Riot Law**.

破壊活動防止法公布。

Subversive Activities Prevention Law enacted.

ヘルシンキの第15回夏季オリンピックに、第2次世界大戦後初めて選手団を送る。

Japan sends a team of athletes, the first in the post–World War II period, to participate in the 15th **Summer Olympic Games** at Helsinki.

フルブライト委員会(日米教育委員会)の奨学制度で、初の日米留学生交換。

First exchange of scholars between Japan and the United States conducted under the auspices of the **Fulbright Commission (Japan-United States Educational Commission)**.

ジャーナリスト松本重治、国際文化会館設立。

International House of Japan founded by the journalist Matsumoto Shigeharu.

内灘事件(1952年～1953年)：石川県内灘の地元民、アメリカ軍の射撃演習場の設置に抗議。

Uchinada Incident (1952–53): villagers in Uchinada, Ishikawa Prefecture, protest the establishment of a US Army firing range.

警察予備隊、保安隊(自衛隊の前身)に改編。

National Police Reserve reorganized as the **National Safety Forces** (forerunner of the **Self Defense Forces**).

1953

テレビ放送はじまる。

Television broadcasting begins in Japan.

公害病の水俣病、第1号患者報告される。

First case of pollution-related **Minamata disease** reported.

1954

平城京(奈良)発掘始まる。

Excavation of the 8th-century imperial palace at Heijōkyō (Nara) begins.

サンフランシスコ平和条約
San Francisco Peace Treaty

ソ連、水爆実験成功を発表。　　　　**1953**
The Soviet Union announces its
successful testing of a hydrogen
bomb.

ダレス国務長官、アメリカの政策・大量　**1954**
報復戦略を発表。
John Foster Dulles announces the US
policy of massive nuclear retaliation.

造船疑獄、第5次吉田茂内閣総辞職。

Shipbuilding Scandal of 1954 contributes to the fall of the fifth Yoshida Shigeru cabinet.

第5福竜丸事件：マーシャル諸島のビキニ島で行われたアメリカの水爆実験による死の灰（放射能灰）で、日本漁船が被爆。

Lucky Dragon **Incident**: Japanese fishing boat contaminated by fallout from a US atomic test on Bikini in the Marshall Islands.

日米相互防衛援助協定調印。

United States-Japan Mutual Defense Assistance Agreement signed.

文部省、外国人留学生の勉学支援のため奨学金制度を設立。

The **Ministry of Education** establishes a scholarship system to support study by foreign students in Japan.

衣笠貞之助の映画「地獄門」、カンヌ映画祭でグランプリ受賞。

Jigokumon (**Gate of Hell**), a film by Kinugasa Teinosuke, receives the Grand Prix at the **Cannes Film Festival**.

防衛庁・自衛隊発足。

Defense Agency and the **Self Defense Forces** established.

1955   第1回原水爆禁止世界大会、広島で開催。

First **Atomic Disasters Anniversary World Conference** against Atomic and Hydrogen Bombs held in Hiroshima.

世界初のトランジスターラジオ、発売される。

First transistor radios go on sale.

日本、**GATT**（関税と貿易に関する一般協定）に加盟。

Japan joins **GATT** (**General Agreement on Tariffs and Trade**).

自由民主党結成。

Liberal Democratic Party formed.

1956   三島由紀夫、小説「金閣寺」を出版。金閣に放火する金閣寺の従弟の心理を描く。

Mishima Yukio publishes the novel *Kinkakuji* (tr *The Temple of the Golden Pavilion*), a psychological portrait of a priest who sets fire to the temple he serves.

槙有恒を隊長とする日本登山隊、ヒマラヤのマナスル初登頂に成功。

Maki Aritsune leads a party of Japanese climbers who make the first ascent of Mt. Manaslu in the Himalayas.

売春防止法公布。

Prostitution Prevention Law passed.

1956年版「経済白書」、「もはや戦後ではない」と宣言。

The 1956 *White Paper on the Economy* declares an "end to the postwar period."

日ソ共同宣言；両国の国交回復。

Soviet-Japanese Joint Declaration reestablishes diplomatic relations between the two countries.

日本、国際連合加盟を認められる。

Japan granted membership in the **United Nations**.

1957   南極観測隊、ベースキャンプ・昭和基地を建設。

Japanese antarctic research expedition establishes **Shōwa Station**, a base camp in Antarctica.

第5福竜丸 **Lucky Dragon**

アメリカ、南ベトナム・カンボジア・ラオスに直接軍事援助を開始。
United States begins providing direct military aid to South Vietnam, Cambodia, and Laos.
ソ連とその衛星国、ワルシャワ条約の下で相互防衛機構を築く。
Mutual defense organization of the Soviet Union and its satellites established under the Warsaw Pact.

1955

昭和基地 **Shōwa Station**

ソ連、初の人工衛星スプートニク1号の打上げに成功。
Soviet Union launches the first space satellite, Sputnik 1.

1957

1958 外国貿易振興のため、**日本貿易振興会**(JETRO)が**通商産業省**の下に設立される。

JETRO, an organization for the promotion of Japan's foreign trade, is established under the administration of the **Ministry of International Trade and Industry**.

東京タワー完成。

Construction of **Tōkyō Tower** completed.

1959 メートル法、日本で公式に採用。

Metric system adopted officially by Japan.

日米安全保障条約改定に反対する抗議始まる。

Beginning of protests against the revision of the **United States-Japan Security Treaty**.

伊勢湾台風、本州中央部を横断；死者・不明約5000人が報告される。

Ise Bay Typhoon crosses central Honshū; some 5,000 people reported dead or missing.

1960 民社党結成。

Democratic Socialist Party formed.

三池争議：三池炭鉱で282日間のストライキ。

Miike strike: 282-day strike at **Miike Coal Mines**.

ワシントンで新**安保条約**調印。条約批准に反対するデモ隊、東京の**国会**を取り囲む。

Second of the **United States-Japan security treaties** signed in Washington; demonstrators against ratification of the treaty besiege the **National Diet Building** in Tōkyō.

日本社会党委員長・浅沼稲次郎、右翼青年に暗殺される。

Japan Socialist Party chairman Asanuma Inejirō assassinated by a right-wing youth.

1961 嶋中事件：狂信的右翼、中央公論社社長嶋中鵬二を暗殺未遂。

Shimanaka Incident: right-wing zealot attempts to murder Shimanaka Hōji, president of the publishing firm Chūō Kōronsha, Inc.

E＝O＝ライシャワー、米国駐日大使となる。

Edwin O. Reischauer becomes United States ambassador to Japan.

1962 安部公房、前衛的小説「砂の女」を出版。

Abe Kōbō publishes the avant-garde novel *Suna no onna* (tr *The Woman in the Dunes*).

サリドマイドの販売停止。

Sale of thalidomide in Japan halted.

1964 東京・大阪間を高速で結ぶ**新幹線**開通。

High-speed Shinkansen (**New Trunk Line**; often called the "**bullet train**") trains begin operations between Tōkyō and Ōsaka.

東京オリンピック：第18回夏季オリンピック大会東京で開催、アジアではじめてのオリンピック。

Tōkyō Olympic Games: eighteenth Summer Olympic Games, the first sponsored by an Asian city, held in Tōkyō.

公明党結成。

Kōmeitō (**Clean Government Party**) formed.

伊勢湾台風 **Ise Bay Typoon**

東京オリンピック
Tōkyō Olimpic Games

石油輸出国機構(OPEC)設立。 Organization of Petroleum Exporting Countries (OPEC) formed.	**1960**
韓国でパクチョンヒ(朴正熙)率いる軍事 評議会、文民政府を倒す。 Military junta led by Pak Chǒng-hǔi and others overthrows the civilian government of South Korea. ベルリンの壁、建設始まる。 Construction of the Berlin Wall begins. 経済協力開発機構(OECD)結成：日本は 1964年に加盟。 Organization for Economic Cooperation and Development (OECD) organized; Japan joins in 1964.	**1961**
アルジェリア、フランスから独立。 Algeria gains independence from France. キューバミサイル危機、ソ連とアメリカ 間に深刻な緊張を引き起こす。 Cuban missile crisis causes acute tension between the Soviet Union and the United States.	**1962**

1965   原水禁(原水爆禁止日本国民会議)結成。
Formation of Gensuikin (**Japan Congress against Atomic and Hydrogen Bombs**).
ベ平連(ベトナムに平和を市民連合)、最初のデモ。
First demonstrations by the **Peace for Vietnam Committee**.
日韓基本条約調印；日韓国交回復。
Korea-Japan Treaty of 1965 signed; diplomatic relations between Japan and the **Republic of Korea** restored.
朝永振一郎、ノーベル物理学賞を共同受賞する。
Tomonaga Shin'ichirō shares the **Nobel Prize for physics**.

1966   遠藤周作、17世紀後半のキリシタン迫害を描いた小説「沈黙」を出版。
Endō Shūsaku publishes the novel *Chimmoku* (tr *Silence*), a depiction of the persecution of Christians in late-17th-century Japan.
ビートルズ、東京の日本武道館で公演；5回のコンサート中、毎回約2000人の警察官が警備にあたる。
The Beatles perform at the Nippon Budōkan in Tōkyō; some 2,000 policemen provide security at each of the five concerts.
井伏鱒二、小説「黒い雨」の連載完了；広島における原子爆弾の恐ろしい影響を描く。
Ibuse Masuji completes serialization of the novel *Kuroi ame* (tr *Black Rain*), a study of the horrific consequences of the atomic bombing at Hiroshima.

1968   大学紛争(1968年〜1969年)はじまる。
University upheavals of 1968–1969 begin.
消費者保護法公布。
Basic Law for Consumer Protection enacted.
アメリカから小笠原諸島返還。
Ogasawara Islands returned to Japanese sovereignty by the United States.
川端康成、ノーベル文学賞受賞。
Kawabata Yasunari wins the **Nobel Prize for literature**.

1969   佐藤・ニクソン共同声明：沖縄の1972年日本返還について合意に達する。
Satō-Nixon Communiqué: agreement reached on the reversion of Okinawa to Japanese sovereignty in 1972.

1970   日本万国博覧会大阪で開催。
EXPO '70 opens in Ōsaka.
日米安全保障条約、自動延長される。
Automatic renewal of the **United States-Japan Security Treaty**.
作家三島由紀夫、極右団体「楯の会」を率いて陸上自衛隊にクーデターを扇動するが、失敗して自殺。
Novelist Mishima Yukio leads his private ultranationalist group Tate no Kai in an attempt to provoke an uprising by Ground Self Defense Forces; failing, he commits suicide.

1971   環境庁設立。
Environment Agency established.
円切上げ(1ドル＝308円)、日本経済の不況を招く。
Revaluation of the yen (¥308 = US $1) depresses the Japanese economy.

アメリカ空軍、北ベトナム空爆開始。
US airplanes begin bombing North Vietnam.

1965

中国で文化大革命広がる。
Cultural Revolution sweeps across China.

1966

朝永振一郎 **Tomonaga Shin'ichirō**

アメリカの宇宙船アポロ11号飛行士、初の月面着陸に成功。
US Apollo 11 spacecraft puts the first man on the moon.

1969

日本万国博覧会 **Expo '70**

1972　札幌で第11回**冬季オリンピック**開催。

The 11th **Winter Olympic Games** held in Sapporo.

連合赤軍浅間山荘事件：軽井沢の浅間山荘で連合赤軍を逮捕の際、警官2
人が殺される；逮捕後の取り調べで内部闘争による仲間14名の処刑が判
明；イスラエルのテルアビのロッド空港で**日本赤軍**乱射事件、死者26人。

United Red Army Asama Lodge Incident: 2 policemen are killed
during an arrest at a lodge in Karuizawa, Nagano Prefecture;
subsequent interrogations reveal 14 other murders committed by
United Red Army members in the course of internal disputes; 26 die
in a **Japanese Red Army** attack on Lod Airport in Tel Aviv, Israel.

アメリカ、沖縄の施政権を日本に返還。

Okinawa returned to Japanese sovereignty by the United States.

日中共同声明；日中国交回復。

China-Japan Joint Communiqué of 1972 issued; it announces the
establishment of diplomatic relations between Japan and the
People's Republic of China.

高松塚古墳発掘；彩色壁画の年代は700年頃にさかのぼる。

Takamatsuzuka tomb excavated; its polychrome wall paintings date
to ca AD 700.

国際交流基金設立。

Japan Foundation established.

1973　円、**変動相場制**に移行。

Floating exchange rate introduced.

田中角栄首相、アメリカの主要大学の日本研究講座に総額1千万ドルを寄付。

Prime Minister Tanaka Kakuei bestows a grant totaling $10 million
on major US universities engaged in Japanese studies.

札幌地方裁判所、**長沼訴訟**で**自衛隊**違憲の判決を下す。(1976年、札幌高
等裁判所判決取り消し)

Sapporo District Court decision in the **Naganuma case** rules the **Self
Defense Forces** to be unconstitutional (reversed by the Sapporo
High Court in 1976).

石油危機：石油価格高騰。

Oil crisis of 1973: oil prices spiral.

江崎玲於奈、ノーベル**物理学賞**を共同受賞。

Esaki Reona shares the **Nobel Prize for physics**.

1974　国土庁設立、国土利用の計画を行う。

National Land Agency established to plan land use.

佐藤栄作前首相、ノーベル**平和賞**受賞。

Former prime minister Satō Eisaku receives the **Nobel Peace Prize**.

田中角栄首相、金脈問題で辞職。

Resignation of Prime Minister Tanaka Kakuei amid allegations of
involvement in financial scandals.

1975　アメリカ大統領G＝R＝フォードの招きで昭和天皇と良子皇后、アメリカを
公式訪問。

At the invitation of US president Gerald R. Ford, Emperor Shōwa
and Empress Nagako make a state visit to the United States.

札幌冬季オリンピック
Sapporo Winter Olympic Games

高松塚古墳 Takamatsuzuka Tomb

アメリカと中国、上海コミュニケで友好
を宣言。
The United States and China
announce rapprochement in the
Shanghai Communiqué.
アメリカとソ連、第1回戦略兵器制限条
約(SALT1)を結ぶ。
The United States and the Soviet
Union conclude the first round of
Strategic Arms Limitation Talks
(SALT I).

1972

江崎玲於奈 **Esaki Reona**

第4次アラブ=イスラエル戦争(中東戦
争)、オイルショックの引き金となる。
Fourth Arab-Israeli War triggers the
oil crisis.

1973

佐藤栄作 **Satō Eisaku**

クメール・ルージュ、プノンペンを占領。
Khmer Rouge take Phnom Penh.
北ベトナム、ベトナム全土を統一。
North Vietnam achieves the
unification of Vietnam.

1975

1976   ロッキード事件：田中角栄前首相、ロッキード社からの収賄罪で逮捕。

Lockheed Scandal: ex-prime minister Tanaka Kakuei charged with taking bribes from Lockheed Aircraft Corporation.

1977   日本、領海12海里・漁業専管水域200海里を実施。

Japan sets its **territorial limit** at 12 **nautical miles** from its coasts and its **fishery zone** at 200 nautical miles from its coasts.

1978   社会民主連合結成。

United Social Democratic Party formed.

新東京国際空港(成田空港)開港。

New Tōkyō International Airport (**Narita Airport**) opens.

日中平和友好条約、調印。

China-Japan Peace and Friendship Treaty signed.

1979   靖国神社戦犯合祀表面化。

It is divulged that convicted **war criminals** are enshrined at **Yasukuni Shrine**.

元号法公布。

Enactment of the **Era Name Law**.

1980   日本の自動車生産台数、アメリカを追い越す。

Japanese automobile production outpaces that of the United States.

1981   厚生省の招きで、中国残留孤児肉親捜しに初来日。

Ministry of Health and Welfare sponsors the visit to Japan of the first group of **displaced Japanese war orphans in China** to search for family members.

福井謙一、ノーベル化学賞を共同受賞。

Fukui Ken'ichi shares the **Nobel Prize for chemistry**.

1982   教科書問題：中国と韓国の政府、日本の歴史教科書の検定に抗議；日本政府は内容の一部訂正に同意。

Textbook issue: Chinese and South Korean governments protest the content of Japanese history textbooks; the Japanese government agrees to revise certain of the disputed passages.

第2次臨時行政調査会、日本の主要3公社の民営化を提案。

Second Provisional Commission for Administrative Reform proposes **privatization** of Japan's three major **public corporations**.

1983   東京ディズニーランド開業。

Tōkyō Disneyland opens.

1984   韓国大統領チョンドファン(全斗煥)、国賓として来日；日韓関係について、昭和天皇は "不幸な過去" に "遺憾の意" を表する。

Korean president **Chŏn Du-hwan** makes state visit to Japan; in reference to Korea-Japan relations, Emperor Shōwa expresses "regret" over the "unfortunate past."

1985   国籍法改正施行；父母両系の血統主義に(片親が日本人であれば、子供の日本国籍取得を認める)。

Amendment to the **Nationality Law** goes into effect; eligibility for Japanese citizenship through either the maternal or paternal line is legally recognized.

日本で最初のエイズ患者、報告される。

First cases of **AIDS** reported in Japan.

新東京国際空港
New Tōkyō International Aiport

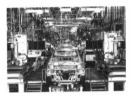

自動車産業 **Automotive Industry**

福井謙一 **Fukui Ken'ichi**

ホメイニ師、イランにイスラム共和国建設。 Ayatollah Ruhollah Khomeini establishes an Islamic republic in Iran. エジプトとイスラエル平和条約に調印。 Peace treaty signed by Egypt and Israel.	1979
イラン・イラク戦争始まる。(1980年〜1988年) Iran-Iraq War commences (1980–88).	1980
中国とイギリス、香港の1997年7月1日中国返還を明記した協定調印を発表。 China and the United Kingdom announce the signing of an agreement stipulating the restoration of Hong Kong to China on 1 July 1997.	1984
ミハイル=ゴルバチョフ、ソビエト共産党書記長に選ばれる。 Mikhail Corbachov elected general secretary of the Communist Party of the Soviet Union.	1985
フェルデイナンド=マルコス追放され、コラソン=アキノがフィリピンの大統領となる。 Ferdinand Marcos is deposed and Corazon Aquino assumes the presidency of the Philippines. ソ連のチェルノブイリ原子力発電所で事故。 Nuclear accident at Chernobyl in the Soviet Union.	1986

男女雇用機会均等法成立、翌年施行。

Enactment of the Equal Employment Opportunity Law for Men and Women; it becomes effective the following year.

中曾根康弘、第2次世界大戦後の首相としてはじめて靖国神社を公式参拝。

Nakasone Yasuhiro becomes the first prime minister since World War II to visit Yasukuni Shrine in his official capacity.

1987 国際日本文化研究センター、京都に設立。

International Research Center for Japanese Studies founded in Kyōto.

利根川進、ノーベル医学・生理学賞受賞。

Tonegawa Susumu wins the **Nobel Prize for physiology and medicine**.

連合(日本労働組合連合)、結成。

Rengō (**Japanese Trade Union Confederation**) formed.

1988 リクルート事件：主要政治家の秘書、1986年にリクルート社から未公開株の譲渡をうけていたことが明るみに出る。

Recruit Scandal: it comes to light that the staffs of a number of leading politicians received gifts of stock shares from Recruit Co in 1986.

消費税、多数派自由民主党により国会を強行採決で通過；翌年、3％の消費税が実施される。

Consumption Tax Law pushed through the Diet by a **Liberal Democratic Party** majority; 3-percent **Consumption Tax** goes into effect the following year.

平成時代 Heisei period (1989–)

1995年8月15日、第2次世界大戦の終戦50周年を迎え、日本の経済・社会は大きな転換期を迎えた。戦後一貫して成長してきた日本経済はバブル崩壊後行き詰まり、戦後かつて経験したことのない不況を経験している。社会は出生率の低下や人口の急速な高齢化など新しい問題に直面している。しかし戦後50年におよぶ民主主義の制度のもと市民社会が成熟し、NPO活動に見られるような新しい力も育って、福祉や国際交流等の分野で大きな力を発揮しはじめた。デジタル技術の進歩や働く女性の著しい増加は、ライフスタイルやビジネス環境に影響を与えはじめている。このなかで日本は行政・金融・教育・福祉等社会のあらゆる分野で戦後制度の改革を進め、21世紀を迎えようとしている。

1989 昭和天皇逝去；天皇明仁即位。

Death of Emperor Shōwa; accession of **Emperor Akihito**.

利根川進 **Tonegawa Susumu**

アメリカ議会、1988年の市民自由法を可決：この法案は、第2次世界大戦中アメリカ政府により強制収容された日系人に公的謝罪と1人当り2万ドルの補償金を明記。

US Congress passes the Civil Liberties Act of 1988; it stipulates that an official apology and $20,000 be given to each Japanese American interned by the US government during World War II.

In the Heisei period, Japan, which observed the fiftieth anniversary of the end of World War II on 15 August 1995, is facing major economic and social challenges. After decades of consistent growth, the excesses of the so-called bubble economy ended in the worst recession of the postwar era. At the same time, Japanese society is facing serious new problems such as a falling birthrate and a rapidly aging population. On the positive side, the civil society nurtured in the 50 years of democracy since 1945 has enabled nonprofit organizations and other groups to focus new resources on tasks such as the promotion of social well-being and international cultural exchange. Developments in digital technology and strong growth in the number of working women are having an increasing effect on lifestyles as well as on the business environment. As it prepares for the 21st century, Japan is moving forward with reforms to postwar era practices in all aspects of society, including government, finance, education, and social welfare.

日米構造協議始まる。

Structural Impediments Initiative Talks between the United States and Japan begin.

総評解散；連合に吸収される。

Sōhyō (**General Council of Trade Unions of Japan**) is disbanded and largely absorbed into Rengō (**Japanese Trade Union Confederation**).

1990

天皇明仁、正式に即位。

Formal enthronement of Emperor Akihito.

ジャーナリスト秋山豊寛、「ソユーズ」TM11号の乗組員に加わる：宇宙に出た最初の日本人。

Journalist Akiyama Toyohiro joins the crew of *Soyuz* TM-11; he is the first Japanese to enter outer space.

1991

日本プロサッカーリーグ(Jリーグ)設立。

Japan Professional Football League ("J League") founded.

1992

国連平和維持活動協力法、6月に国会を通過；自衛隊員、海外で平和維持活動に参加する事が可能になる。

Law on Cooperation in United Nations Peacekeeping Operations passed by the Diet in June; Japanese **Self Defense Forces** personnel are permitted to participate in peacekeeping operations in foreign lands.

アメリカのスペースシャトル「エンデバー」2号打ち上げ：初の日本人宇宙飛行士毛利衛乗船。

The American space shuttle *Endeavor II* is launched; among those aboard is Japan's first professional astronaut, Mōri Mamoru.

天皇明仁と皇后美智子、天皇夫妻として初めて中国を公式訪問。

Emperor Akihito and **Empress Michiko** make their first official visit to China as emperor and empress.

1993

環境基本法制定：公害対策基本法(1967年)に代わって環境保全と自然保護を推進。

Enactment of the **Basic Environment Law** for the protection of the environment and **conservation**. It replaces the **Pollution Countermeasures Basic Law** (1967).

ウルグアイ=ラウンドの合意に基づき、日本米市場の開放を決定。

Japan accepts partial opening of the **rice market** based on an agreement reached at the **Uruguay Round**.

非自民連立内閣成立；38年に及ぶ自民党支配終わる。

Non-LDP **coalition government** is formed, marking the end of the LDP's 38 years in power.

1994

政治改革関連法案国会通過：衆議院に小選挙区比例代表制導入される。

Political reform bills pass in the Diet: the **single-seat constituency and proportional representation system** is introduced into the House of Representatives.

関西国際空港開港。

Kansai International Airport opens.

大江健三郎、ノーベル文学賞受賞。

Ōe Kenzaburō awarded the **Nobel Prize for literature**.

天皇明仁 **Emperor Akihito**

天安門事件；中国の民主化を求めるデモ
隊を軍隊が制圧、死者多数。
Tiananmen Square Incident;
thousands of demonstrators for
democratization in China are killed
by government troops in and around
the square.
ベトナム、カンボジアから最後の兵力を
撤退。
Vietnam withdraws the last of its
forces form Cambodia.
ベルリンの壁崩壊。
Berlin Wall demolished.

1989

イラク、クエート侵攻：湾岸戦争始まる
(1990年〜1991年)。
Persian Gulf War commences with
Iraq's invasion of Kuwait (1990–91).
東西ドイツ統一。
Reunification of Germany.

1990

ワルシャワ条約機構、解体。
Warsaw Treaty Organization
dissolved.
南北朝鮮、国連に承認される。
North and South Korea admitted to
the United Nations.
ソビエト連邦解体。
Soviet Union dissolved.

1991

カンボジア国連暫定政府(UNTAC)、明
石康の指揮下で活動開始。
United Nations Transitional
Authority in Cambodia (UNTAC)
begins operations under the
leadership of Akashi Yasushi.
国連環境開発会議(UNCED)、リオデジ
ャネイロで開かれる。
United Nations Conference on
Environment of Development
(UNCED) held in Rio de Janeiro.

1992

欧州連合条約(マーストリヒト条約)発効。
Treaty on European Union (Treaty of
Maastricht) becomes effective.

1993

大江健三郎 **Ōe Kenzaburō**

1995 阪神淡路大震災：マグニチュード7.2、死者6,000人を超える。

Kōbe Earthquake; this magnitude 7.2 earthquake results in more than 6,000 deaths.

地下鉄サリン事件：オウム真理教毒ガスサリンをまく。乗客・駅員12人が死亡、5500人以上が重軽傷。

Subway Sarin Gas Incident: 12 passengers and train attendants die, and over 5,500 people are injured by sarin nerve gas released by the Aum religious sect.

1996 薬害エイズ事件：厚生省、血友病患者の**HIV感染**の法的責任を認める。

AIDS Scandal: the Ministry of Health and Welfare admits its legal responsibility for failing to prevent **HIV infection** among hemophiliacs.

民主党結成。

Democratic Party formed.

1997 介護保険制度成立：2000年から実施。

Long-term-care insurance system established; to go into effect in 2000.

日米防衛協力の指針公表。

Guidelines for US-Japan Defense Cooperation issued.

地球温暖化防止京都会議（「気候変動枠組み条約」第3回締約国会議）開催。

Kyōto Conference on Global Warming (Third Session of the Conference of the Parties to the United Nations Framework Convention on Climate Change: COP3) held in Kyōto.

1998 山一證券廃業、北海道拓殖銀行業務停止。

Yamaichi Securities and **Hokkaidō Takushoku Bank** go bankrupt.

長野で第18回冬季オリンピック開催。

The 18th **Winter Olympic Games** held in Nagano.

金融監督庁発足。

Financial Supervisory Agency established.

(株)日本長期信用銀行・(株)日本債券信用銀行、一時国有化される。

Long-Term Credit Bank of Japan, Ltd, and **Nippon Credit Bank, Ltd,** are temporarily placed under state control.

1999 1997年の臓器移植法施行後はじめての脳死移植行われる。

Organ transplant from a brain dead donor is performed as allowed by the **Organ Transplant Law** enacted in 1997.

阪神淡路大震災 **Kōbe Earthquake**

地下鉄サリン事件
Subway Sarin Gas Incident

GATTに代わり世界貿易機関(WTO)発足。

World Trade Organization (WTO) established as a replacement for GATT.

1995

付録
APPENDIX

天皇表
Emperors and Reigning Empresses

代 Number in traditional count	天皇 Sovereign		生没年 Birth and death dates	在位 Reign dates	即位 Year of enthronement[1]
1	神武	Jimmu[2]			
2	綏靖	Suizei[2]			
3	安寧	Annei[2]			
4	懿徳	Itoku[2]			
5	孝昭	Kōshō[2]			
6	孝安	Kōan[2]			
7	孝霊	Kōrei[2]	legendary emperors		
8	孝元	Kōgen[2]			
9	開化	Kaika[2]			
10	崇神	Sujin[2]			
11	垂仁	Suinin[2]			
12	景行	Keikō[2]			
13	成務	Seimu[2]			
14	仲哀	Chūai[2]			
15	応神	Ōjin[2]	late 4th to early 5th century		
16	仁徳	Nintoku[2]			
17	履中	Richū[2]	first half of the 5th century		
18	反正	Hanzei[2]			
19	允恭	Ingyō[2]			
20	安康	Ankō[2]	mid-5th century		
21	雄略	Yūryaku[2]			
22	清寧	Seinei[2]			
23	顕宗	Kenzō[2]	latter half of the 5th century		
24	仁賢	Ninken[2]			
25	武烈	Buretsu[2]			
26	継体	Keitai[2]			
27	安閑	Ankan[2]	first half of the 6th century		
28	宣化	Senka[2]			
29	欽明	Kimmei	509–571	531 or 539 to 571	
30	敏達	Bidatsu	538–585	572–585	
31	用明	Yōmei	?–587	585–587	
32	崇峻	Sushun	?–592	587–592	
*33	推古	Suiko	554–628	593–628	
34	舒明	Jomei	593–641	629–641	
*35	皇極	Kōgyoku[3]	594–661	642–645	
36	孝徳	Kōtoku	597–654	645–654	
*37	斉明	Saimei	594–661	655–661	
38	天智	Tenji	626–672	661–672	668
39	弘文	Kōbun	648–672	672	

代 Number in traditional count		天皇 Sovereign	生没年 Birth and death dates	在位 Reign dates	即位 Year of enthronement[1]
40	天武	Temmu	?–686	672–686	673
*41	持統	Jitō	645–703	686–697	690
42	文武	Mommu	683–707	697–707	
*43	元明	Gemmei	661–721	707–715	
*44	元正	Genshō	680–748	715–724	
45	聖武	Shōmu	701–756	724–749	
*46	孝謙	Kōken[4]	718–770	749–758	
47	淳仁	Junnin	733–765	758–764	
*48	称徳	Shōtoku	718–770	764–770	
49	光仁	Kōnin	709–782	770–781	
50	桓武	Kammu	737–806	781–806	
51	平城	Heizei	774–824	806–809	
52	嵯峨	Saga	786–842	809–823	
53	淳和	Junna	786–840	823–833	
54	仁明	Nimmyō	810–850	833–850	
55	文徳	Montoku	827–858	850–858	
56	清和	Seiwa	850–881	858–876	
57	陽成	Yōzei	869–949	876–884	877
58	光孝	Kōkō	830–887	884–887	
59	宇多	Uda	867–931	887–897	
60	醍醐	Daigo	885–930	897–930	
61	朱雀	Suzaku	923–952	930–946	
62	村上	Murakami	926–967	946–967	
63	冷泉	Reizei	950–1011	967–969	
64	円融	En'yū	959–991	969–984	
65	花山	Kazan	968–1008	984–986	
66	一条	Ichijō	980–1011	986–1011	
67	三条	Sanjō	976–1017	1011–1016	
68	後一条	Go-Ichijō	1008–1036	1016–1036	
69	後朱雀	Go-Suzaku	1009–1045	1036–1045	
70	後冷泉	Go-Reizei	1025–1068	1045–1068	
71	後三条	Go-Sanjō	1034–1073	1068–1073	
72	白河	Shirakawa	1053–1129	1073–1087	
73	堀河	Horikawa	1079–1107	1087–1107	
74	鳥羽	Toba	1103–1156	1107–1123	1108
75	崇徳	Sutoku	1119–1164	1123–1142	
76	近衛	Konoe	1139–1155	1142–1155	
77	後白河	Go-Shirakawa	1127–1192	1155–1158	
78	二条	Nijō	1143–1165	1158–1165	1159
79	六条	Rokujō	1164–1176	1165–1168	
80	高倉	Takakura	1161–1181	1168–1180	
81	安徳	Antoku[5]	1178–1185	1180–1185	
82	後鳥羽	Go-Toba	1180–1239	1183–1198	1184

代 Number in traditional count	天皇 Sovereign		生没年 Birth and death dates	在位 Reign dates	即位 Year of enthronement[1]
83	土御門	Tsuchimikado	1195–1231	1198–1210	
84	順徳	Juntoku	1197–1242	1210–1221	1211
85	仲恭	Chūkyō	1218–1234	1221	
86	後堀河	Go-Horikawa	1212–1234	1221–1232	1222
87	四条	Shijō	1231–1242	1232–1242	1233
88	後嵯峨	Go-Saga	1220–1272	1242–1246	
89	後深草	Go-Fukakusa	1243–1304	1246–1260	
90	亀山	Kameyama	1249–1305	1260–1274	
91	後宇多	Go-Uda	1267–1324	1274–1287	
92	伏見	Fushimi	1265–1317	1287–1298	1288
93	後伏見	Go-Fushimi	1288–1336	1298–1301	
94	後二条	Go-Nijō	1285–1308	1301–1308	
95	花園	Hanazono	1297–1348	1308–1318	
96	後醍醐	Go-Daigo	1288–1339	1318–1339	
97	後村上	Go-Murakami	1328–1368	1339–1368	
98	長慶	Chōkei	1343–1394	1368–1383	
99	後亀山	Go-Kameyama	?–1424	1383–1392	
N1	光厳	Kōgon	1313–1364	1331–1333	1332
N2	光明	Kōmyō	1322–1380	1336–1348	1338
N3	崇光	Sukō	1334–1398	1348–1351	1350
N4	後光厳	Go-Kōgon	1338–1374	1351–1371	1354
N5	後円融	Go-En'yū	1359–1393	1371–1382	1375
100	後小松	Go-Komatsu[6]	1377–1433	1382–1412	1392
101	称光	Shōkō	1401–1428	1412–1428	1415
102	後花園	Go-Hanazono	1419–1471	1428–1464	1430
103	後土御門	Go-Tsuchimikado	1442–1500	1464–1500	1466
104	後柏原	Go-Kashiwabara	1464–1526	1500–1526	1521
105	後奈良	Go-Nara	1497–1557	1526–1557	1536
106	正親町	Ōgimachi	1517–1593	1557–1586	1560
107	後陽成	Go-Yōzei	1572–1617	1586–1611	1587
108	後水尾	Go-Mizunoo	1596–1680	1611–1629	
*109	明正	Meishō	1624–1696	1629–1643	1630
110	後光明	Go-Kōmyō	1633–1654	1643–1654	
111	後西	Gosai	1637–1685	1655–1663	1656
112	霊元	Reigen	1654–1732	1663–1687	
113	東山	Higashiyama	1675–1710	1687–1709	
114	中御門	Nakamikado	1702–1737	1709–1735	1710
115	桜町	Sakuramachi	1720–1750	1735–1747	
116	桃園	Momozono	1741–1762	1747–1762	
*117	後桜町	Go-Sakuramachi	1740–1813	1762–1771	1763
118	後桃園	Go-Momozono	1758–1779	1771–1779	
119	光格	Kōkaku	1771–1840	1780–1817	
120	仁孝	Ninkō	1800–1846	1817–1846	

代 Number in traditional count	天皇 Sovereign		生没年 Birth and death dates	在位 Reign dates	即位 Year of enthronement[1]
121	孝明	Kōmei	1831–1867	1846–1867	1847
122	明治	Meiji	1852–1912	1867–1912	1868
123	大正	Taishō	1879–1926	1912–1926	1915
124	昭和	Shōwa	1901–1989	1926–1989	1928
125	今上	*kinjō*	1933–	1989–	1990
		(present emperor, Emperor Akihito)			

* 女帝

Indicates empress.

N 南北朝時代の北朝天皇。

Emperors of the Northern Court during the period of the Northern and Southern Courts.

[1] 即位年は在位開始年より1年またはそれ以上遅れた場合のみ記載。

Year of formal enthronement when later than first year of actual reign.

[2] 第1代～14代天皇は伝承上の天皇とみなされている。

The first 14 sovereigns are considered legendary rather than historical.

[3] 第35代皇極天皇、第37代斉明天皇として重祚。

Kōgyoku (35) later reigned as Saimei (37).

[4] 第46代孝謙天皇、第48代称徳天皇として重祚。

Kōken (46) later reigned as Shōtoku (48).

[5] 源平の争乱末期、第81代安徳天皇は平氏の都落ちに従う。対立する源氏は後鳥羽天皇を擁立。このため両天皇の在位期間が一時重複。

During the last phase of the Taira-Minamoto War, Antoku (81) fled the capital with the Taira, and Go-Toba (82) was installed as rival emperor by the Minamoto; their reign dates thus overlap.

[6] 1382年から北朝第6代天皇。1392年南朝吸収後も天皇として在位。

Sixth emperor of the Northern Court from 1382, sole emperor from 1392.

注 NOTE

この表の生没年や在位期間は、日本で使われていた太陰太陽暦を西洋の太陽暦に厳密に比定しました。このため一般に用いられている年代と異なる場合があります。

The life and reign dates in this table have been carefully corrected for discrepancies between the Japanese lunisolar (or lunar-solar) and Western solar calendars. In some instances they may differ from the tables in standard Japanese reference works.

年号表
Table of Japanese Era Names (Nengō)

年号 Japanese era name		西暦 Western calendar	年号 Japanese era name		西暦 Western calendar
大化	Taika	645–650	応和	Ōwa	961–964
白雉	Hakuchi	650–654	康保	Kōhō	964–968
(白鳳	Hakuhō	672–685)	安和	Anna	968–970
朱鳥	Shuchō	686	天禄	Tenroku	970–973
		(686–687)			(970–974)
大宝	Taihō	701–704	天延	Ten'en	973–976
慶雲	Keiun	704–708			(974–976)
和銅	Wadō	708–715	貞元	Jōgen	976–978
霊亀	Reiki	715–717	天元	Tengen	978–983
養老	Yōrō	717–724	永観	Eikan	983–985
神亀	Jinki	724–729	寛和	Kanna	985–987
天平	Tempyō	729–749	永延	Eien	987–989
天平感宝	Tempyō Kampō	749	永祚	Eiso	989–990
天平勝宝	Tempyō Shōhō	749–757	正暦	Shōryaku	990–995
天平宝字	Tempyō Hōji	757–765	長徳	Chōtoku	995–999
天平神護	Tempyō Jingo	765–767	長保	Chōhō	999–1004
神護景雲	Jingo Keiun	767–770	寛弘	Kankō	1004–1012
宝亀	Hōki	770–781			(1004–1013)
天応	Ten'ō	781–782	長和	Chōwa	1012–1017
延暦	Enryaku	782–806			(1013–1017)
大同	Daidō	806–810	寛仁	Kannin	1017–1021
弘仁	Kōnin	810–824	治安	Jian	1021–1024
天長	Tenchō	824–834	万寿	Manju	1024–1028
承和	Jōwa	834–848	長元	Chōgen	1028–1037
嘉祥	Kashō	848–851	長暦	Chōryaku	1037–1040
仁寿	Ninju	851–854	長久	Chōkyū	1040–1044
斉衡	Saikō	854–857	寛徳	Kantoku	1044–1046
天安	Ten'an	857–859	永承	Eijō	1046–1053
貞観	Jōgan	859–877	天喜	Tengi	1053–1058
元慶	Gangyō	877–885	康平	Kōhei	1058–1065
仁和	Ninna	885–889	治暦	Jiryaku	1065–1069
寛平	Kampyō	889–898	延久	Enkyū	1069–1074
昌泰	Shōtai	898–901	承保	Jōhō	1074–1077
延喜	Engi	901–923	承暦	Jōryaku	1077–1081
延長	Enchō	923–931	永保	Eiho	1081–1084
承平	Jōhei	931–938	応徳	Ōtoku	1084–1087
天慶	Tengyō	938–947	寛治	Kanji	1087–1094
天暦	Tenryaku	947–957			(1087–1095)
天徳	Tentoku	957–961	嘉保	Kahō	1094–1096

年号 Japanese era name		西暦 Western calendar	年号 Japanese era name		西暦 Western calendar
		(1095–1097)	承元	Jōgen	1207–1211
永長	Eichō	1096–1097	建暦	Kenryaku	1211–1213
		(1097)			(1211–1214)
承徳	Jōtoku	1097–1099	建保	Kempō	1213–1219
康和	Kōwa	1099–1104			(1214–1219)
長治	Chōji	1104–1106	承久	Jōkyū	1219–1222
嘉承	Kajō	1106–1108	貞応	Jōō	1222–1224
天仁	Tennin	1108–1110	元仁	Gennin	1224–1225
天永	Ten'ei	1110–1113	嘉禄	Karoku	1225–1227
永久	Eikyū	1113–1118			(1225–1228)
元永	Gen'ei	1118–1120	安貞	Antei	1227–1229
保安	Hōan	1120–1124			(1228–1229)
天治	Tenji	1124–1126	寛喜	Kangi	1229–1232
大治	Daiji	1126–1131	貞永	Jōei	1232–1233
天承	Tenshō	1131–1132	天福	Tempuku	1233–1234
長承	Chōshō	1132–1135	文暦	Bunryaku	1234–1235
保延	Hōen	1135–1141	嘉禎	Katei	1235–1238
永治	Eiji	1141–1142	暦仁	Ryakunin	1238–1239
康治	Kōji	1142–1144	延応	En'ō	1239–1240
天養	Ten'yō	1144–1145	仁治	Ninji	1240–1243
久安	Kyūan	1145–1151	寛元	Kangen	1243–1247
仁平	Nimbyō	1151–1154	宝治	Hōji	1247–1249
久寿	Kyūju	1154–1156	建長	Kenchō	1249–1256
保元	Hōgen	1156–1159	康元	Kōgen	1256–1257
平治	Heiji	1159–1160	正嘉	Shōka	1257–1259
永暦	Eiryaku	1160–1161	正元	Shōgen	1259–1260
応保	Ōho	1161–1163	文応	Bun'ō	1260–1261
長寛	Chōkan	1163–1165	弘長	Kōchō	1261–1264
永万	Eiman	1165–1166	文永	Bun'ei	1264–1275
仁安	Nin'an	1166–1169	建治	Kenji	1275–1278
嘉応	Kaō	1169–1171	弘安	Kōan	1278–1288
承安	Jōan	1171–1175	正応	Shōō	1288–1293
安元	Angen	1175–1177	永仁	Einin	1293–1299
治承	Jishō	1177–1181	正安	Shōan	1299–1302
養和	Yōwa	1181–1182	乾元	Kengen	1302–1303
寿永	Juei	1182–1185	嘉元	Kagen	1303–1306
元暦	Genryaku	1184–1185			(1303–1307)
文治	Bunji	1185–1190	徳治	Tokuji	1306–1308
建久	Kenkyū	1190–1199			(1307–1308)
正治	Shōji	1199–1201	延慶	Enkyō	1308–1311
建仁	Kennin	1201–1204	応長	Ōchō	1311–1312
元久	Genkyū	1204–1206	正和	Shōwa	1312–1317
建永	Ken'ei	1206–1207	文保	Bumpō	1317–1319

年号 Japanese era name		西暦 Western calendar	年号 Japanese era name		西暦 Western calendar
元応	Gen'ō	1319–1321	享徳	Kyōtoku	1452–1455
元亨	Genkō	1321–1324	康正	Kōshō	1455–1457
正中	Shōchū	1324–1326	長禄	Chōroku	1457–1460
嘉暦	Karyaku	1326–1329			(1457–1461)
元徳	Gentoku	1329–1332	寛正	Kanshō	1460–1466
元弘	Genkō	1331–1334			(1461–1466)
建武	Kemmu	1334–1338	文正	Bunshō	1466–1467
(南朝 Southern Court)			応仁	Ōnin	1467–1469
延元	Engen	1336–1340	文明	Bummei	1469–1487
興国	Kōkoku	1340–1346	長享	Chōkyō	1487–1489
		(1340–1347)	延徳	Entoku	1489–1492
正平	Shōhei	1346–1370	明応	Meiō	1492–1501
		(1347–1370)	文亀	Bunki	1501–1504
建徳	Kentoku	1370–1372	永正	Eishō	1504–1521
文中	Bunchū	1372–1375	大永	Taiei	1521–1528
天授	Tenju	1375–1381	享禄	Kyōroku	1528–1532
弘和	Kōwa	1381–1384	天文	Tembun	1532–1555
元中	Genchū	1384–1392	弘治	Kōji	1555–1558
(北朝 Northern Court)			永禄	Eiroku	1558–1570
正慶	Shōkyō	1332–1333	元亀	Genki	1570–1573
暦応	Ryakuō	1338–1342	天正	Tenshō	1573–1592
康永	Kōei	1342–1345			(1573–1593)
貞和	Jōwa	1345–1350	文禄	Bunroku	1592–1596
観応	Kannō	1350–1352			(1593–1596)
文和	Bunna	1352–1356	慶長	Keichō	1596–1615
延文	Embun	1356–1361	元和	Genna	1615–1624
康安	Kōan	1361–1362	寛永	Kan'ei	1624–1644
貞治	Jōji	1362–1368			(1624–1645)
応安	Ōan	1368–1375	正保	Shōhō	1644–1648
永和	Eiwa	1375–1379			(1645–1648)
康暦	Kōryaku	1379–1381	慶安	Keian	1648–1652
永徳	Eitoku	1381–1384	承応	Jōō	1652–1655
至徳	Shitoku	1384–1387	明暦	Meireki	1655–1658
嘉慶	Kakyō	1387–1389	万治	Manji	1658–1661
康応	Kōō	1389–1390	寛文	Kambun	1661–1673
明徳	Meitoku	1390–1394	延宝	Empō	1673–1681
(南北朝合一 Northern and Southern Courts unified 1392)			天和	Tenna	1681–1684
応永	Ōei	1394–1428	貞享	Jōkyō	1684–1688
正長	Shōchō	1428–1429	元禄	Genroku	1688–1704
永享	Eikyō	1429–1441	宝永	Hōei	1704–1711
嘉吉	Kakitsu	1441–1444	正徳	Shōtoku	1711–1716
文安	Bun'an	1444–1449	享保	Kyōhō	1716–1736
宝徳	Hōtoku	1449–1452	元文	Gembun	1736–1741

年号 Japanese era name		西暦 Western calendar		年号 Japanese era name		西暦 Western calendar
寛保	Kampō	1741–1744		弘化	Kōka	1844–1848
延享	Enkyō	1744–1748				(1845–1848)
寛延	Kan'en	1748–1751		嘉永	Kaei	1848–1854
宝暦	Hōreki	1751–1764				(1848–1855)
明和	Meiwa	1764–1772		安政	Ansei	1854–1860
安永	An'ei	1772–1781				(1855–1860)
天明	Temmei	1781–1789		万延	Man'en	1860–1861
寛政	Kansei	1789–1801		文久	Bunkyū	1861–1864
享和	Kyōwa	1801–1804		元治	Genji	1864–1865
文化	Bunka	1804–1818		慶応	Keiō	1865–1868
文政	Bunsei	1818–1830		明治	Meiji	1868–1912
		(1818–1831)		大正	Taishō	1912–1926
天保	Tempō	1830–1844		昭和	Shōwa	1926–1989
		(1831–1845)		平成	Heisei	1989–

注 NOTE

この表では、1873年1月1日に西暦が採用される以前の年号に2つの異なる西暦が入っている場合があります。上段は日本で広く一般に用いられている西暦です。下段の括弧内は、旧暦と西暦の年初のずれを厳密に考慮して換算したものです。

For some eras prior to the adoption of the Western calendar on 1 January 1873, two sets of dates are given. In these cases the first set are the commonly accepted dates that appear in most standard Japanese reference works. The second set of dates (in parentheses) have been converted precisely from the old Japanese lunisolar calendar to account for discrepancies between it and the Western solar calendar as to when a new year begins.

国・都道府県図
The Traditional Provinces and the Modern Prefectures

国名(824年～1868年)　Provinces, 824–1868

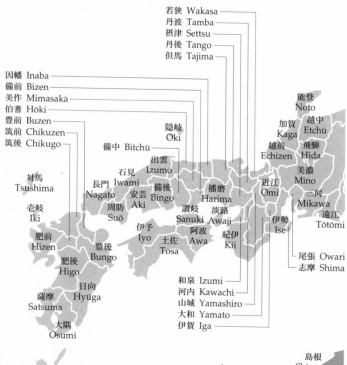

若狭　Wakasa
丹波　Tamba
摂津　Settsu
丹後　Tango
但馬　Tajima

因幡　Inaba
備前　Bizen
美作　Mimasaka
伯耆　Hōki
豊前　Buzen
筑前　Chikuzen
筑後　Chikugo

隠岐　Oki

能登　Noto
加賀　Kaga
越中　Etchū
越前　Echizen
飛騨　Hida

備中　Bitchū

出雲　Izumo
石見　Iwami
長門　Nagato
安芸　Aki
周防　Suō

備後　Bingo

播磨　Harima
淡路　Awaji

近江　Omi
美濃　Mino
三河　Mikawa
遠江　Tōtōmi

対馬　Tsushima
壱岐　Iki
肥前　Hizen
肥後　Higo

伊予　Iyo
土佐　Tosa
讃岐　Sanuki
阿波　Awa
紀伊　Kii

伊勢　Ise

豊後　Bungo
日向　Hyūga
薩摩　Satsuma
大隅　Ōsumi

尾張　Owari
志摩　Shima

和泉　Izumi
河内　Kawachi
山城　Yamashiro
大和　Yamato
伊賀　Iga

島根　Shimane
山口　Yamaguchi
広島　Hiroshima
福岡　Fukuoka
佐賀　Saga
長崎　Nagasaki
大分　Oita
愛媛　Ehime
熊本　Kumamoto
宮崎　Miyazaki
鹿児島　Kagoshima

注 **NOTE**

隠岐島、佐渡島、対馬はそれぞれ一国を形成していたが、現在は島根県、新潟県、長崎県の一部。北海道と沖縄は前近代の国郡制には含まれていなかった。

The islands of Oki, Sado, and Tsushima, formerly provinces, are now part of Shimane, Niigata, and Nagasaki prefectures, respectively. Neither Hokkaidō nor Okinawa was included in the premodern provincial system.

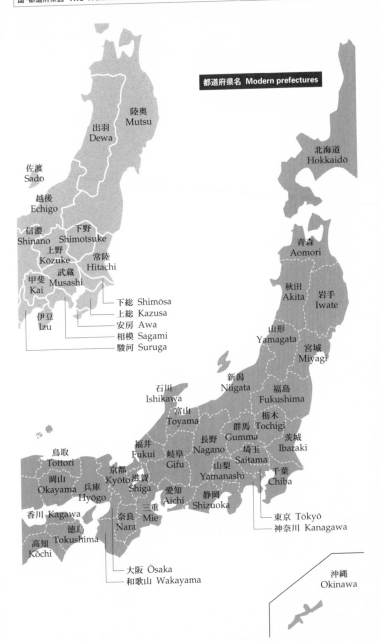

都道府県名 Modern prefectures

江戸幕府主要職制表
Principal Officials of the Edo Shogunate

将軍 shogun

- 大老 *tairō* (great elder)
- 老中 *rōjū* (senior councillors)
- 奏者番 *sōshaban* (masters of shogunal ceremony)
- 寺社奉行 *jisha bugyō* (commissioners of temples and shrines)
- 京都所司代 Kyōto *shoshidai* (Kyōto deputy)
- 大坂城代 Ōsaka *jōdai* (keeper of Ōsaka Castle)
- 側用人 *sobayōnin* (grand chamberlain)

- 若年寄 *wakadoshiyori* (junior councillors)

  - 江戸町奉行 Edo machi *bugyō* (Edo city commissioners)
  - 勘定奉行 *kanjō bugyō* (commissioners of finance)
    - 代官 *daikan* (intendants)
  - 勘定吟味役 *kanjō gimmiyaku* (comptrollers)
  - 大目付 *ōmetsuke* (inspectors general)
  - 遠国奉行 *ongoku bugyō* (commissioners of distant provinces)
  - 大番頭 *ōbangashira* (captains of the great guard)
  - 留守居 *rusui* (keepers of Edo Castle)
  - 禁裏付 *kinrizuki* (envoys to the court)
  - 高家 *kōke* (masters of court ceremony)
  - 側衆 *sobashū* (chamberlains)

  - 小姓頭取、小納戸頭取 *koshō tōdori* and *konando tōdori* (chiefs of the pages and attendants)
  - 目付 *metsuke* (inspectors)
  - 書院番頭、小姓組番頭、新番頭 *shoimban-gashira, koshōgumiban-gashira,* and *shimban-gashira* (captains of the bodyguard, inner guard, and new guard)

譜代大名から任命。

These positions were held by *fudai* (hereditary vassal) *daimyō*.

行政府組織図
Organization of the Executive Branch of the Government (March 1999)

内閣 Cabinet
- 内閣官房 Cabinet Secretariat
- 内閣法制局 Cabinet Legislation Bureau
- 安全保障会議 Security Council of Japan
- 人事院 National Personnel Authority

総理府 Prime Minister's Office
- 公正取引委員会 Fair Trade Commission
- 国家公安委員会 National Public Safety Commission
- 公害等調整委員会 Environmental Disputes Coordination Commission
- 宮内庁 Imperial Household Agency
- 総務庁 Management and Coordination Agency
- 北海道開発庁 Hokkaidō Development Agency
- 防衛庁 Defense Agency
- 防衛施設庁 Defense Facilities Administration Agency
- 経済企画庁 Economic Planning Agency
- 科学技術庁 Science and Technology Agency
- 環境庁 Environment Agency
- 沖縄開発庁 Okinawa Development Agency
- 国土庁 National Land Agency

外務省 Ministry of Foreign Affairs

建設省 Ministry of Construction

郵政省 Ministry of Posts and Telecommunications

法務省 Ministry of Justice
- 司法試験管理委員会 National Bar Examination Administration Commission
- 公安審査委員会 Public Security Examination Commission
- 公安調査庁 Public Security Investigation Agency

大蔵省 Ministry of Finance
- 国税庁 National Tax Administration

文部省 Ministry of Education
- 文化庁 Agency for Cultural Affairs

厚生省 Ministry of Health and Welfare
- 社会保険庁 Social Insurance Agency

農林水産省 Ministry of Agriculture, Forestry, and Fisheries
- 食糧庁 Food Agency
- 林野庁 Forestry Agency
- 水産庁 Fisheries Agency

通商産業省 Ministry of International Trade and Industry
- 資源エネルギー庁 Agency for Natural Resources and Energy
- 特許庁 Patent Office
- 中小企業庁 Small and Medium Enterprise Agency

運輸省 Ministry of Transport
- 船員労働委員会 Central Labor Relations Commission for Seafarers
- 海上保安庁 Maritime Safety Agency
- 海難審判庁 High Marine Accidents Inquiry Agency
- 気象庁 Meteorological Agency

労働省 Ministry of Labor
- 中央労働委員会 Central Labor Relations Commission

自治省 Ministry of Home Affairs
- 消防庁 Fire Defense Agency

会計検査院 Board of Audit

暦
Calendar and Dates

　日本が現在の太陽暦(グレゴリオ暦)を採用したのは1873年(明治6年)1月1日からで、月日の数え方は欧米と同じになったが、年の数え方は、西暦と共に年につける名(年号)も併用している。年号の歴史は古く、645年の政治改革を記念した大化に始まる。その後わずかの空白があるものの、大宝(701年～703年)以降は連続して現在に至っている。年号は明治以降一世一元となり天皇一代に一年号となったが、それ以前は祥瑞、災異などさまざまな理由で改元が頻繁に行われていた。

　1873年以前は太陰太陽暦を採用していた。太陰太陽暦の歴史は古く推古天皇のころから使用していたとされ、中国から朝鮮半島を経由して伝えられた。正式に暦が採用された記録があるのは持統天皇の時で690年である。

　太陰太陽暦とは生活の中で比較的わかりやすい月の満ち欠けによる1月と農耕には不可欠の1太陽年とをうまくかみ合わせて、季節と毎年の日付ができるだけ一致するように作られたものである。月は地球のまわりを約30日弱で一周するが新月、つまり太陽と月が同じ方向にあるとき、を朔といい、満月、つまり太陽と月が地球をはさんで正反対の方向にあるとき、を望といい朔から次の朔までを1朔望月という。現在では平均値で29.530589日とされている。太陰太陽暦の仕組みは、基本的には一月を29日(小の月)と30日(大の月)とし平年を354日あるいは355日とし(353日、356日もある)、不足する10日余りを調整するために2～3年に1度、正確には19年に7回閏月という月を挿入し、一年を384日(383日、385日もある)とするものである。その閏月挿入の根拠となり太陽暦と結びつけているものが二十四節気であり一年を12等分にしその節目を節気と呼びその中間点を中気と呼びそれぞれ名称がある。月の決め方はその12の中気がある月をその名で呼ぶ。例えば正月中(雨水)がある朔望月を正月つまり一月という。であるから、立春が前年になったりもする。

　二十四節気は冬至を起点に一年365.2422日を12等分した約30.44日を足していきその中間点を計算する方法(常気という)と太陽の黄経30度ごとに割り出す方法(定気という)があるが、天保暦以来現在でも定気を採用している。この一年の12等分が一朔望月より長いため中気のない朔望月がでてくるのでその月を閏月としている。

Since 1 January 1873 (Meiji 6), the Japanese have used the Gregorian calendar, and the modern Japanese method of designating dates does not differ from the Western one except that, in addition to the Western designations for years, the Japanese continue to use the relatively brief calendrical eras known as *nengō* (e.g., the year 1999 is also known as Heisei 11).

Nengō

The practice of using era names to designate years, which originated in China, has a long history in Japan. The first Japanese era name, commemorating the revolutionary political changes of AD 645, was Taika, or Great Reform. Except for a brief lapse in the latter part of the 7th century, *nengō* have been in continuous use ever since. Beginning with the Meiji era in 1868, the current practice, in which the entire reign of an emperor corresponds to one era, was adopted. Before that, era names had been changed more frequently and for a variety of reasons, as on some auspicious occasion or after some felicitous or unlucky event.

The Premodern Calendar

Before 1873, the official Japanese calendar was a lunisolar (or lunar-solar) calendar, in other words, a combination of a lunar calendar, in which the months are reckoned by the phases of the moon, with a solar one, in which the year is measured by the natural progression of the seasons. This system, which came to Japan from China by way of the Korean peninsula, is traditionally said to have first been used in Japan during the reign of Empress Suiko

(593–628); however, the first record of its official adoption refers to the year 690, during the reign of Empress Jitō (686–697).

The combined lunisolar calendar provided an easily understood way of determining the months, as the phases of the moon were a part of everyday life, and at the same time it gave farmers the (solar) division of the year into seasons that they needed in order to know the best times for planting and for harvests. However, in order for a calendar year to contain a whole number of months, the year calculated in lunar months deviated considerably from the solar, or natural, year, and certain adjustments were necessary to assure that there would be a rough correspondence between a certain month of the calendar year and a certain season of the natural year. Lunar, or synodic, months (sakubōgetsu) were reckoned from one new moon to the next, with a new moon occurring on the first day of the month. Such a month contains 29.530589 days, and the months were adjusted to give each a whole number of days (either 29 or 30). A 12-month year in this system normally contained either 354 or 355 days (some years contained either 353 or 356), which was more than 10 days short of the natural year. In order to adjust for this discrepancy, an intercalary month (uruuzuki) was inserted in some years. To insert a 13th month in every year would have given the year more days than the natural year; however, it was discovered that by inserting an intercalary month in 7 years out of every 19 (the metonic cycle), an overall adjustment could be achieved.

Intercalation of additional months was determined with reference to the 24 seasonal points that divided the solar year and that were known as sekki and chūki, there being 12 of each. These seasonal divisions thus served to integrate the lunar and solar aspects of the calendar. The solar year was divided into 12 equal divisions (about 30.44 days) called setsu. The beginning of a setsu was known as a sekki, and the midpoint of a setsu was called a chūki. Each sekki and chūki had its own name, often highly expressive of weather or agricultural phenomena. (These 24 points—the Nijūshisekki—in the old Japanese calendar correspond very closely to dates of the Gregorian calendar. The Gregorian date corresponding to the Japanese New Year varied, but it was always between 21 January and 19 February.) The method for determining intercalary months was as follows. It was the chūki that were used to determine the names (numbers) of the months, from 1 to 12. Some lunar months contained no chūki because the number of days in a lunar month was less than the number of days between two chūki. (If a chūki fell a few hours immediately before a full moon, the next chūki would fall just after the next new moon.) In such a case, the whole intervening lunar month between the two chūki was called intercalary (uruu) and took its name (number) from the preceding month.

二十四節気(1999年) The 24 Points (sekki and chūki): 1999

節気・中気 Sekki or chūki	名称 Name	解説 Associations	太陽黄経 Celestial longitude	中央標準時 Japanese standard time (time) (dates)	
12月節 December setsu	小寒 Shōkan	寒さ増す Cold weather increases	285°	04:17	6 Jan.
12月中 December chū	大寒 Daikan	寒気最も厳しいころ Maximum winter cold	300°	21:37	20 Jan.
正月節 January setsu	立春 Risshun	春来る Beginning of spring	315°	15:57	4 Feb.
正月中 January chū	雨水 Usui	雪、雨に変わる Snow turns to rain	330°	11:47	19 Feb.

節気・中気 Sekki or chūki	名称 Name	解説 Associations	太陽黄経 Celestial longitude	中央標準時 Japanese standard time (time)	(dates)
2月節 February *setsu*	啓蟄 Keichitsu	暖かさに虫はい出す Warmer weather; insects emerge	345°	09:58	6 Mar.
2月中 February *chū*	春分 Shumbun	春分 Vernal equinox	0°	10:46	21 Mar.
3月節 March *setsu*	清明 Seimei	東南の風さわやかな季はこぶ Southeasterly winds bring pleasant weather	15°	14:45	5 Apr.
3月中 March *chū*	穀雨 Kokuu	春雨に穀物芽ぶく Grains germinate in spring rains	30°	21:46	20 Apr.
4月節 April *setsu*	立夏 Rikka	夏来る Beginning of summer	45°	08:01	6 May
4月中 April *chū*	小満 Shōman	草木生い茂る All things growing	60°	20:52	21 May
5月節 May *setsu*	芒種 Bōshu	田植のころ Rice transplanting	75°	12:09	6 Jun.
5月中 May *chū*	夏至 Geshi	夏至 Summer solstice	90°	04:49	22 Jun.
6月節 June *setsu*	小暑 Shōsho	暑さ増す Summer heat increases	105°	22:25	7 Jul.
6月中 June *chū*	大暑 Taisho	暑気最も厳しいころ Maximum summer heat	120°	15:44	23 Jul.
7月節 July *setsu*	立秋 Risshū	秋来る Beginning of autumn	135°	08:14	8 Aug.
7月中 July *chū*	処暑 Shosho	秋風吹き暑さやわらぐ Autumn winds bring a lessening of heat	150°	22:51	23 Aug.
8月節 August *setsu*	白露 Hakuro	秋の気配、鳥わたる Autumn weather; birds migrate	165°	11:10	8 Sep.
8月中 August *chū*	秋分 Shūbun	秋分 Autumnal equinox	180°	20:31	23 Sep.
9月節 September *setsu*	寒露 Kanro	木々紅葉して秋たけなわ Leaves turn color; the height of autumn	195°	02:48	9 Oct.
9月中 September *chū*	霜降 Sōkō	初霜、秋終る First frost; the end of autumn	210°	05:52	24 Oct.
10月節 October *setsu*	立冬 Rittō	冬来る Beginning of winter	225°	05:58	8 Nov.
10月中 October *chū*	小雪 Shōsetsu	小雪舞う Light snowfall	240°	03:25	23 Nov.
11月節 November *setsu*	大雪 Taisetsu	大雪降り真冬となる Heavy snowfall; winter weather	255°	22:47	7 Dec.
11月中 November *chū*	冬至 Tōji	冬至 Winter solstice	270°	16:44	22 Dec.

出典 Source：「理科年表」 *Rika nempyō*

日本語索引
Japanese Index

す

ち

つ

て

と

英語索引
English Index

バイリンガル日本史年表
Chronology of Japanese History

1999年7月9日　第1刷発行

編　著　　講談社インターナショナル株式会社

発行者　　野間佐和子

発行所　　講談社インターナショナル株式会社
　　　　　〒112-8652　東京都文京区音羽1-17-14
　　　　　電話：03-3944-6493（編集部）
　　　　　　　　03-3944-6492（業務部・営業部）

印刷所　　大日本印刷株式会社

製本所　　大日本印刷株式会社